MONSTERS WHO
MURDER

MONSTERS WHO MURDER

TRUE STORIES OF THE WORLD'S MOST EVIL SERIAL KILLERS

AL CIMINO

This edition published in 2023 by Arcturus Publishing Limited
26/27 Bickels Yard, 151–153 Bermondsey Street,
London SE1 3HA

AD010937UK

Printed in the UK

CONTENTS

CONTENTS

INTRODUCTION

Most of us are very fortunate. During our lifetimes, we have little or no contact with murder. We don't do it, we don't suffer it – not even at second hand through the loss of family or friends if we're lucky. However, a huge amount of literature, film and TV is given over to homicide. Like it or not, it seems we are fascinated by it.

Of course, most of the media output concerning murder is anodyne – Agatha Christie, *Midsomer Murders*, Sherlock Holmes, *Colombo*. The motives are straightforward – a disputed will, jealousy, a business deal gone wrong. However, in real life the motive for murder is rarely so sanitary and straightforward. And yet, the pages of newspapers and books are filled with the details of the most brutal, inhuman homicides.

One step beyond are the tales of those who kill and kill again. Serial killers are particularly captivating because they are unfathomable. Even serial rapist-killers are unDarwinian, though their motivation might appear purely sexual. How can the perpetrator's genes hope to replicate if the unwilling recipient is dead?

But the motivation of a serial killer is rarely that uncomplicated. Indeed, part of the fascination is the imaginative attempt we all make, from a safe distance, to get inside the mind of serial killers. What makes them tick? What is the gratification they seek from taking another person's life? What makes it so compelling is that they do it over and over again, even though they know they are very likely to get caught and the outcome will almost certainly be incarceration for life or execution. Some of them, towards the end of a 'successful' career as a serial killer, almost welcome getting caught.

There is another draw that serial killers have on our imaginations. Although we all know that a certain amount of conformity is necessary for society to function, most of us have a sneaking admiration for the outlaw, those who take on life on their own terms. While that can indeed be admirable in the arts and other intellectual pursuits – even in business and politics – the serial killer is the ultimate outlaw. Serial killers break all the rules.

That is not to stick up for them. They are despicable people. It would be better for everyone if they did not exist. You wouldn't want to know one – beyond in the movies, on TV or in the pages of a book like this one.

There are 27 real-life case histories within these pages. I hope you find them as fascinating as I do. And I should add what has now become the obligatory warning. There are scenes in this book that some readers may find distressing, but read on anyway.

Al Cimino
Bloomsbury, January 2023

JEFFREY DAHMER: THE MILWAUKEE CANNIBAL

Milwaukee mass murderer Jeffrey Dahmer kept the corpses of his victims around his home. But it wasn't enough. He wanted to possess them even more completely, so he ended up eating their flesh. That way they would be a part of him and stay with him forever.

Dahmer began his murderous career at the age of 18 in 1978. At that time, his parents were going through an acrimonious divorce. Dahmer's father had already left and his mother was away on a vacation. Dahmer was alone in the house and feeling very neglected, so he went out looking for company. He picked up a hitch-hiker, a 19-year-old white youth named Steven Hicks, who had spent the day at a rock concert. They got on well and Dahmer took Hicks back to his parents' house. They had a few beers and talked about their lives. Then Hicks said that he had to go. Dahmer begged him to stay, but Hicks was insistent, so Dahmer made him stay. He picked up a heavy dumbbell, clubbed him around the head and strangled him.

Dahmer dragged Hicks's body into the crawlspace under the house and dismembered it using a hunting knife. He had had plenty of practice. His childhood hobby had been dissecting animals. He wrapped the body parts in plastic bags and stashed them there. But the stench of rotting flesh soon permeated the house. At night, Dahmer took the remains and buried them in a nearby wood. Soon he became afraid that local children would discover the grave, so he dug up the body parts, stripped off the flesh and pulverized the bones with a sledgehammer. Then he scattered the pieces around his garden and on neighbouring property. It was almost ten years before Dahmer killed again.

In December 1981, Dahmer moved to Milwaukee, Wisconsin to live with his grandmother. He was a loner. He would hang out in gay bars. If he did strike up a conversation with another customer, he would slip drugs into their drink. Often, they would end up in a coma. Dahmer made no attempt to rape them; he was simply experimenting. But when the owner of the Club Bar ended up unconscious in hospital, Dahmer was barred.

In 1986, Dahmer was sentenced to a year's probation for exposing himself and masturbating publicly in front of two 12-year-old boys. He claimed he was urinating and promised the judge that it wouldn't happen again.

Six days after the end of his probation in November 1987, he picked up 24-year-old Stephen Tuomi in a gay club. They went to the Ambassador Hotel to have sex. When Dahmer awoke, he found Tuomi dead. There was blood around his mouth and bruising around his neck.

Dahmer had been drunk the night before and realized that he must have strangled Tuomi. Now he was alone in a hotel room with a corpse and any minute the porter would be checking whether the room had been vacated. He rushed out and bought a large suitcase. He stuffed Tuomi's body into it and took a taxi back to his grandmother's house. The taxi driver even helped him drag the heavy case inside. Dahmer then cut up the body and put the bits into plastic bags, which he put out for the garbage collectors. He performed this task so well that he left no traces at all. When the police called around to ask him about the disappearance of Tuomi, there was no sign of the body. Dahmer found that he had got away with his second murder.

Twisted mind

Sex, companionship and death were now inextricably linked in Dahmer's mind. Four months later, he picked up a 14-year-old Native American male prostitute named James Doxtator, offering him $50 to pose nude for him. They went back to Dahmer's grandmother's house and had sex in the basement. Dahmer gave the boy a drink laced with a powerful sedative. When Doxtator was unconscious, he strangled him. He dismembered the corpse, stripped off the flesh, pulverized the bones and scattered the pieces.

Two months later, Dahmer met a 22-year-old bisexual, Richard Guerrero, who was broke. Dahmer offered him money to perform in a video. He had oral sex with Dahmer in his grandmother's basement. When it was over, Dahmer offered him a drink, drugged him, strangled him and disposed of the corpse after performing oral sex on it.

Dahmer's grandmother began to complain of the smell that persisted even after the garbage had been collected. She found a patch of blood in the garage. Dahmer said that he had been skinning animals out there. She accepted this excuse but made it clear that she wanted him to move out.

Dahmer found himself a small apartment in a run-down, predominantly black area. On his first night there, he lured Keison

Sinthasomphone, a 13-year-old Laotian boy, back to the flat and drugged him. The boy, whose older brother later perished at Dahmer's hands, somehow managed to escape. Dahmer was arrested and charged with sexual assault and enticing a minor for immoral purposes. He spent a week in jail, then was released on bail.

Grisly souvenirs

By this time, Dahmer could not contain his compulsion to kill. While out on bail, he picked up handsome 26-year-old black bisexual, Anthony Sears. Fearing that the police were watching his apartment, he took Sears back to his grandmother's basement. They had sex, then Dahmer drugged him, killed him and dismembered his body. He disposed of Sears's corpse in the garbage, but kept his skull and genitals as souvenirs.

Back in court, the District Attorney pushed for five years' imprisonment for his assault on 13-year-old Keison Sinthasomphone. Dahmer's attorney argued that the attack was a one-off offence. His client, he said, was a homosexual and a heavy drinker, and needed psychiatric help, not punishment. Dahmer got five years on probation and a year on a correction programme.

It did not help. Dahmer was now set in his murderous ways. He picked up a young black stranger in a club and offered him money to pose for nude photographs. Back in Dahmer's flat, the youth accepted a drink. It was drugged. When he lapsed into unconsciousness, Dahmer strangled him, stripped him and performed oral sex on the corpse. Then he dismembered the body, again keeping the skull, which he painted grey.

He picked up another notorious homosexual known as 'the Sheikh' and did the same to him – only this time he performed oral sex before he drugged and strangled his victim.

The next victim, a 15-year-old Hispanic, was luckier. Dahmer offered him $200 to pose nude. He undressed, but Dahmer neglected to drug him before attacking him with a rubber mallet. Dahmer tried to strangle him, but he fought back. Eventually Dahmer calmed down. The boy promised not to inform the police and Dahmer let him go. Dahmer even called him a taxi.

Next day, when he went to hospital for treatment, the boy broke his promise and spoke to the police. But he begged them not to let his foster parents find out that he was homosexual and the police dropped the matter altogether.

The next time Dahmer picked up a victim, a few weeks later, he craved more than the usual sex, murder and grisly dismemberment. He decided to keep the skeleton. He dissolved most of the flesh in acid, but kept the biceps intact in the fridge.

When neighbours began to complain about the smell of putrefying flesh coming from Dahmer's flat, Dahmer apologized. He said that the fridge was broken and he was waiting to get it fixed.

Grotesque photographs

Dahmer's next victim, 23-year-old David Thomas, was not gay. He had a girlfriend and a three-year-old daughter but accepted Dahmer's offer to come back to his apartment for money. After drugging him, Dahmer realized that he did not really fancy his latest pick-up anyway. But fearing that Thomas might make trouble when he woke up, he killed him. This time he took more pleasure in the dismemberment, photographing it step by step.

Nineteen-year-old aspiring model Curtis Straughter was engaged in oral sex with Dahmer when the sleeping potion took effect. Dahmer strangled him and, again, photographed the dismemberment. Once again, his skull was kept as a trophy.

Nineteen-year-old Errol Lindsey's murder proceeded along exactly the same lines. Dahmer offered him money to pose for nude photographs, drugged, strangled and dismembered him. The grisly process was again recorded photographically and his skull was added to Dahmer's collection.

Thirty-one-year-old deaf mute, Tony Hughes, also accepted $50 to pose nude. But by this time, Dahmer had become so blasé about the whole procedure that he kept Hughes's body in his bedroom for several days before he cut it up.

Dahmer's next victim was Keison Sinthasomphone's older brother, 14-year-old Konerak. Again, things went badly wrong. Dahmer drugged the boy, stripped him and raped him, but then, instead of strangling him, Dahmer went out to buy some beer. On his way back to the apartment, Dahmer saw Konerak out on the street. He was naked, bleeding and talking to two black girls. When Dahmer grabbed him, the girls hung on to him. One of them had called the police and two patrol cars arrived.

The police wanted to know what all the trouble was about and Dahmer said that he and Konerak had had a lovers' tiff. He managed to convince them that 14-year-old Konerak was really 19 and, back at his apartment, showed them Polaroids of Konerak in his underwear to back up his story that they were lovers. The police did not realize that the pictures had been taken earlier that day, while Konerak was drugged.

Throughout all this, Konerak sat passively on the sofa, thinking his ordeal was over. In fact, it had only just begun. The police accepted Dahmer's story and left. Konerak was strangled immediately and then dismembered. The three policemen responsible were later dismissed.

Just one more drink

Dahmer attended Gay Pride Day in Chicago and, on the way back, picked up another would-be model, Matt Turner. Back at Dahmer's apartment, he was strangled and dismembered.

Jeffrey Dahmer

When Dahmer picked up 23-year-old Jeremiah Weinberger in a gay club, Weinberger asked his former roommate whether he should go with him. The roommate said: 'Sure, he looks okay.'

Dahmer seems to have liked Weinberger. They spent the whole of the next day together having sex. Then Weinberger looked at the clock and said it was time to go – and Dahmer said he should stay for just one more drink. His head ended up next to Matt Turner's in the freezer.

When Dahmer lost his job, he knew only one thing would make him feel better. He picked up a 24-year-old black man called Oliver Lacy, took him back to his apartment, strangled him and sodomized his dead body.

Four days later, 25-year-old Joseph Bradeholt – who was married with two children – accepted Dahmer's offer of money to pose for nude photographs and willingly joined in oral sex with him, according to Dahmer. His dismembered torso was left to soak in a dustbin filled with acid.

Complacent killer

By the time Dahmer had killed 17 men, all in much the same way, he was getting so blasé that it was inevitable he would get caught. On 22 June 1991, Dahmer met Tracy Edwards, a young black man who had just arrived from Mississippi. He was with a number of friends. Dahmer invited them all back to his apartment for a party. He said he and Edwards would go ahead in a taxi and organize some beers. The others would follow later. Edwards went along with this plan. What he did not know was that Dahmer gave his friends the wrong address.

Edwards did not like Dahmer's apartment. It smelt funny. There was a fish tank, where Dahmer kept some Siamese fighting fish. Dahmer told lurid tales about the fish fighting to the death and Edwards glanced nervously at the clock as he sipped his cold beer.

When the beer was finished, Dahmer gave Edwards a rum and coke. It was drugged. Edwards became drowsy. Dahmer put his arms around him and whispered about going to bed. Instantly, Edwards was wide awake. It was all a mistake. He had to be going, he said.

Before he knew it, he was handcuffed and Dahmer was poking a butcher's knife in his chest, ordering him to get undressed. Edwards realized the seriousness of his situation. He knew he had to humour the man and make him relax. Slowly, he unbuttoned his shirt.

Dahmer suggested that they go through into the bedroom and escorted Edwards there at knifepoint. The room was decorated with Polaroid pictures of young men posing naked. There were other pictures of dismembered bodies and chunks of meat. The smell in the room was sickening. The putrid aroma seemed to be coming from a plastic dustbin under the window. Edwards could guess the rest.

Dahmer wanted to watch a video with his captive friend. They sat on the bed and watched *The Exorcist*. The gruesome movie made Dahmer relax and Edwards thought of ways to escape.

If Edwards did not comply with his requests, Dahmer said, he would rip out his heart and eat it. Then he told Edwards to strip, so that he could photograph him nude. As Dahmer reached for the camera, Edwards seized his opportunity. He punched him in the side of the head. As Dahmer went down, Edwards kicked him in the stomach and ran for the door.

Dahmer caught up with him and offered to unlock the handcuffs, but Edwards ignored him. He wrenched open the door and ran for his life.

Halfway down 25th Street, Edwards spotted a police car. He ran over to it yelling for help. In the car, he explained to the officer that a maniac had tried to kill him and he directed them back to Dahmer's apartment.

Strange smell

The door was answered by a well-groomed white man who seemed calm and composed. The police began to have second thoughts about the story Edwards had told them – until they noticed the strange smell.

Dahmer admitted that he had threatened Edwards. He looked contrite and explained that he had just lost his job and had been drinking. But when the police asked for the key to the handcuffs, he refused to hand it over and grew violent. The policemen pushed him back into the flat and, in moments, had him face down on the floor. They read him his rights. Then they began looking around the flat. One of them opened the fridge door.

'Oh my God,' he said, 'there's a goddamn head in here.'

Dahmer began to scream like an animal. The police rushed out to get some shackles. Then, they began their search of the apartment in earnest.

The refrigerator contained meat, including a human heart, in plastic bags. There were three human heads in the freezer. A filing cabinet contained bizarre photographs, three human skulls and a collection of bones. Two more skulls were found in a pot on the stove. Another pot contained male genital organs and severed hands, and there were the remains of three male torsos in the dustbin in the bedroom.

At the precinct, Dahmer seemed almost relieved that his murder spree was over. He made a detailed confession and admitted that he had now reached the stage where he was cooking and eating his victims' bodies.

Dahmer's cannibalism and his necrophilia were the cornerstones of his plea of insanity. But the district attorney pointed out to the jury that, if Dahmer were found insane and sent to a mental hospital, his case would be reviewed in two years and, if he was then found sane, he could be out on the streets again. The jury found Jeffrey Dahmer guilty of the 15 murders he was charged with and he was given 15 life sentences. The state of Wisconsin has no death penalty.

Three months after he had been sentenced in Milwaukee, Dahmer was extradited to Ohio where he pleaded guilty to the murder of his first victim, Steven Hicks, and was given another life sentence. He was then sent back to the Columbia Correctional Institution in Wisconsin where he was baptized into the Church of Christ. He was slashed with a razor while sitting in the chapel. Then on 28 November 1994, Jeffrey Dahmer was bludgeoned to death in the showers by another inmate.

'Now is everybody happy? Now that he's bludgeoned to death, is that good enough for everyone?' said his mother. Four hundred people held a candlelight vigil in Milwaukee to celebrate.

HENRY LEE LUCAS: AMERICA'S MOST PROLIFIC SERIAL KILLER

Thought to be America's most prolific serial killer, Henry Lee Lucas had a partner in crime. With his accomplice, Ottis Toole, he confessed to over 360 murders – 157 of these confessions have been checked out by the authorities and proved to be genuine.

Lucas's mother was half-Chippawa. She was drunk most of the time on corn liquor which she bought with the proceeds of prostitution, conducted on the floor of her shack in front of her husband and children. She was known to be 'as mean as a rattlesnake' and packed the seven children from her first marriage off to a foster home. Lucas's father worked on the railways and lost both legs in an accident.

Lucas's mother and her pimp beat her children constantly. After one beating, Henry was unconscious for three days and suffered damage to his brain. Another accident left him with a glass eye.

Henry was made to grow his hair long and wear a dress, so that he could be pimped out to both men and women. The county court put an end to this forced cross-dressing when his school complained.

At the age of ten, Henry Lucas was introduced to sex by Bernard Dowdy, yet another of his mother's lovers. Dowdy was mentally retarded. He would slit the throat of a calf and have sex with the carcass; he encouraged the boy to do the same. Lucas enjoyed this activity and, from childhood onwards, he associated sex with death.

Throughout his childhood Lucas continued to have sex with animals, sometimes skinning them alive for sexual pleasure. At 14, he turned his perverted attention to women. He beat a 17-year-old girl unconscious at a bus stop and raped her. When she came to and started screaming, he choked the life out of her, or so he claimed.

At 15, he was sent to a reformatory for burglary. Two years of hard labour on a prison farm did nothing to reform him. When he was released, he returned to housebreaking. He was caught again and sent back to jail.

He escaped, then met and fell in love with a girl called Stella. They stayed together for four years and she agreed to marry him. Then his mother turned up demanding that her son take care of her. After a violent row, Lucas killed her. This time he got 40 years, but served just ten.

By 1970, the authorities considered Lucas a reformed character and released him. He killed a woman within hours of getting out. In 1971, he was arrested for attempting to rape two teenage girls at gunpoint. His only excuse was that he craved women all the time.

Feeding the flame

Released in 1975, he married a woman called Betty Crawford. The marriage broke up when Betty discovered that he was having sex with her nine-year-old daughter and trying to force himself on her seven-year-old. Lucas then moved in with his sister but was thrown out when he started having sex with her daughter too.

In 1978, he met another sex-murder freak called Ottis Toole in a soup kitchen in Jacksonville, Florida. He was a sadist with homosexual tendencies. He often dressed as a woman to pick up men in bars. He even started a course of female hormones as part of his ambition to have a sex change. Toole was also a pyromaniac and would achieve orgasm at the sight of a burning building.

Lucas and Toole became lovers and together they embarked on a series of violent robberies, which frequently involved murder – often for the sheer pleasure of it. In Toole's confession, he admitted that, around that time, they saw a teenage couple walking along a road after their car had run out of petrol. Toole shot the boy, while Lucas forced the girl into the back of the car. After he had finished raping her, he shot her six times and they dumped her body by the roadside. This was one of the cases the police could confirm.

Another killing occurred outside Oklahoma City. There, they had picked up a girl called Tina Williams when her car broke down. Lucas shot her twice and had sex with her dead body.

In 1978, Lucas and Toole were in Maryland when a man asked them whether they would help him transport stolen cars. This was too tame a sport for hardened criminals such as them, they explained. He then asked them whether they were interested in becoming professional killers. They said that they were. The one proviso was that they had to join a Satanist cult.

Lucas and Toole claimed to have been inducted into the Hand of Death sect in Florida by a man named Don Meteric. As part of the initiation, Lucas had to kill a man. He lured the victim to a beach and gave him a bottle of whisky. When the man threw his head back to take a swig, Lucas cut his throat.

As part of the cult activity, Lucas and Toole kidnapped young prostitutes who were forced to perform in pornographic videos, which often turned out to be 'snuff movies'. They also abducted children and took them across the border into Mexico where they were sold or used as sacrifices in satanic ceremonies. These children may have been delivered to Adolfo de Jesus Constanzo, the bisexual high priest, and his one-time lover, the beautiful, American-college-educated Sara Maria Aldrete, known as *La Bruja* – 'The Witch'. They murdered and mutilated children in Mexico during satanic rites. Their victims' genitals were cut out and their brains boiled. The flesh of 'gringos' was especially in demand.

Murderous rampage

Around that time, Toole introduced Lucas to his 11-year-old niece, Becky Powell, who was slightly mentally retarded. She lived in Toole's mother's house in Florida where they were staying. Toole had been seduced by his older sister Druscilla, before he became a homosexual, and he enjoyed watching his pick-ups make love to Becky or her older sister Sarah.

When Druscilla committed suicide, Becky and her brother Frank were put in care. Lucas decided to rescue them. By January 1982, they were on the run together, living off the money they stole from small grocery stores. Becky called Lucas 'Daddy'. But one night, when he was tickling her innocently at bedtime, they began to kiss. Lucas undressed her, then stripped off himself. Becky was only 12, he said, but she looked 18.

During his time with Becky, Lucas continued his murderous rampage with Toole. Lucas outlined a typical fortnight in Georgia. In the space of two weeks, they kidnapped and murdered a 16-year-old girl, then raped her dead body, and abducted, raped and mutilated a blond woman. Another woman was abducted from a parking lot and stabbed to death in front of her children. In the course of one robbery, the store owner was shot. Another man died in a second robbery. In a third, the store owner was stabbed. And in a fourth, a woman was tied up before being stabbed to death. Toole also tried to force his sexual

Henry Lee Lucas.

attentions on a young man. On being spurned, Toole shot him. Becky and her brother Frank were often in on the robberies and witnessed several of the murders.

Eventually, Lucas and Toole parted company. Toole took Frank back to Florida, while Lucas and Becky got a job with a couple named Smart who ran an antique shop in California. After five months, the Smarts sent Lucas and Becky to Texas to look after Mrs Smart's 80-year-old mother, Kate Rich.

A few weeks later, Mrs Smart's sister visited her mother to find the place filthy. Lucas had been taking her money to buy beer and cigarettes. She found him drunk in bed with Becky and the two of them were fired.

They were hitch-hiking out of town when they were picked up by the Reverend Reuben Moore, who had started a religious community nearby called the House of Prayer. Lucas and his 15-year-old common-law wife quickly became converts and lived in a converted chicken barn. While they were staying at the House of Prayer, Becky seems to have had a genuine change of heart. She was homesick and she wanted to go back to Florida. Reluctantly, Lucas agreed and they set off hitch-hiking.

At nightfall, they settled down with their blankets in a field. It was a warm June night. A row broke out about Becky's decision to return home. She struck him in the face. He grabbed a knife and stabbed her through the heart. Then he had sex with her corpse, cut her body up and scattered its dismembered pieces in the woods.

After killing Becky, who Lucas later described as the only woman he had ever loved, he returned to the House of Prayer. He, too, seems to have had some sort of change of heart. One Sunday, he dropped around to Mrs Rich's house to offer her a lift to church. She accepted. But during the journey, she began to question him about the whereabouts of Becky. Lucas pulled a knife and stabbed it into her side. She died immediately. He drove her to a piece of waste ground where he undressed and raped her corpse. He stuffed her naked body into a drainage pipe that ran under the road. Later, he collected it in a garbage bag and burned it in the stove at the House of Prayer.

Sheriff Bill F. 'Hound Dog' Conway of Montague County, Texas, had begun to have his suspicions about Lucas when he reappeared without Becky. Now he was linked to the disappearance of two women. Lucas was hauled in for questioning.

Under pressure

Lucas was a chain-smoker and heavy caffeine addict. Conway deprived him of both cigarettes and coffee, but still he refused to break. Lucas maintained that he knew nothing about the disappearance of Kate Rich, and that Becky had run off with a truck driver who promised to take her back to Florida. Finally, Sheriff Conway had to release him.

Soon afterwards, Lucas told the Reverend Moore that he was going off to look for Becky. He headed for Missouri, where he saw a young woman standing beside her car in a petrol station. He held a knife to her ribs and forced her back into the car. They drove south towards Texas. When she dozed off, Lucas pulled off the road with the intention of raping her. She awoke suddenly to find a knife at her neck. He stabbed her in the throat, pushed her to the ground and cut her clothes off. After he had raped her dead body, he dragged it into a copse and took the money from her handbag. He abandoned her car in Fredericksburg, Texas and returned to the House of Prayer.

While he was away, the Reverend Moore had told Sheriff Conway that Lucas had given Becky a gun for safekeeping. Lucas was a convicted felon and had, consequently, forfeited his right to bear arms. It was enough to put him back in the slammer. Sheriff Conway again deprived him of coffee and cigarettes. This time, Lucas began to crack. He was found hanging in his cell with his wrists slashed.

After being patched up in the prison hospital, Lucas was put in a special observation cell in the women's wing. The next night, he cracked completely. In the early hours of the morning, he started yelling. When the jailer arrived, Lucas claimed that there was a light in his cell and it was talking to him. The man on night duty, Joe Dan Weaver, knew that Lucas had already smashed the bulb in his cell and told him to get some sleep. Later in the night, Lucas called the jailer again and confessed that he had done some pretty bad things. Weaver advised him to get down on his knees and pray. Instead, Lucas asked Weaver for a pencil and paper.

Lucas spent the next half hour writing a note to Sheriff Conway. It read: 'I have tried to get help for so long, and no one will believe me. I have killed for the past ten years and no one will believe me. I cannot go on doing this. I have killed the only girl I ever loved.'

When the confession was finished, Lucas pushed it out of the cell door's peep hole. Weaver read it and called Sheriff Conway. He knew the sheriff would not mind being woken in the middle of the night under these circumstances.

When Sheriff Conway arrived, he plied Lucas with coffee and cigarettes – and asked about the murders. Lucas said that he had seen a light in his cell and it had told him to confess his sins. Then he told the sheriff that he had killed Kate Rich.

Later, Sheriff Conway and Texas Ranger Phil Ryan asked Lucas what had happened to Becky Powell. Tears flowed from his one good eye as Lucas told how he had stabbed, raped and dismembered her. The story left the two hardened law officers feeling sick and wretched.

'Is that all?' ask Ryan wearily, half-hoping it was.

'Not by a long way,' said Lucas. 'I reckon I killed more than 100.'

Litany of horror

The next day Montague County police began to check out Lucas's story. Near the drainage pipe where Lucas had temporarily hidden Mrs Rich's body, they found some of her underclothes and her glasses, broken. At the House of Prayer, they found some burnt fragments of human flesh and some charred bones.

Lucas took them to the field where he had killed Becky. They found her suitcase, full of women's clothing and make-up. Her skull, pelvis and other parts of her body were found in the woodland nearby, in an advanced stage of decomposition.

He began to confess to other murders too – often in breathtaking detail. These too checked out.

A week after he had begun to confess, Lucas appeared in court, charged with the murders of Kate Rich and Becky Powell. When asked whether he understood the seriousness of the charges against him, Lucas said he did and confessed to about 100 other murders.

The judge, shocked, could scarcely credit this and asked Lucas whether he had ever undergone psychiatric examination. Lucas said he had, but 'they didn't want to do anything about it ... I know it ain't normal for a person to go out and kill girls just to have sex.'

Lucas's sensational testimony made huge headlines and the news wires quickly carried the story to every paper in the country. Police departments in every state and county began checking their records and Lucas's confessions were run through the computer at the newly established National Center for the Analysis of Violent Crime.

Toole, it was discovered, was already in prison. He had been sentenced to 15 years for arson in Springfield. In jail, he had begun regaling a cellmate with the tale of how he had raped, murdered, beheaded, barbecued and eaten a child named Adam Walsh. Suddenly, in the light of Lucas's confession, the police began taking his stories seriously.

Both Lucas and Toole continued to confess freely. They admitted to a series of robberies of convenience stores. At one, they had tied up a young girl. She had wriggled free, so Lucas had shot her in the head and Toole had had sex with her dead body.

Lucas went on a thousand-mile tour of murder sites. In Duval Country, Florida, Lucas confessed to eight unsolved murders. The victims had been women ranging in age from 17 to 80. Some had been beaten, some strangled, some stabbed and some shot. Lucas said that the Hand of Death said he should vary his MO.

Near Austin, Texas, Lucas pointed out a building and asked whether it had been a liquor store once. It had. Lucas confessed to murdering the former owners during a robbery in 1979. In the same county, Lucas led them to a field where he had murdered and mutilated a girl called Sandra Dubbs. He even pointed out where her car had been found.

Lucas and Toole had cruised Interstate 35, murdering tramps, hitch-hikers, men who were robbed of their money and old women who were abducted from their homes. They had killed more than 20 people up and down that highway alone, over a period of five years. One was a young woman who was found near Austin, naked except for a pair of orange socks. She had been hitch-hiking on the interstate when

Lucas had picked her up. She refused to have sex with him, so Lucas strangled her and took what he wanted. She was never identified, but Lucas was sentenced to death for her murder. Although he withdrew his confession to the Becky Powell murder and pleaded not guilty, he was found guilty anyway and sentenced to life. On top of that he received four more life sentences, two sentences of 75 years each and one of 67 years, all for murder.

During his confessions, Lucas told the police that Toole had poured petrol over a 65-year-old man and set him alight. They had hidden, so that they could watch the fire engines arrive. The police identified the man as George Sonenberg. He had died four days later. Until then, they had assumed that the fire was an accident. Toole freely admitted the murder and claimed to have started hundreds of other fires. But it was for this particularly horrific murder that Toole, as well, was sentenced to death.

Lucas and Toole enjoyed their brief celebrity and took a certain relish in revealing the ghoulish details of their shocking crimes. Both their death sentences were commuted. Toole died of cirrhosis at the Florida State Prison on 15 September 1996 at the age of 49. His body went unclaimed and he was buried in the prison cemetery. Lucas died of heart failure on 12 March 2001, aged 64, in the Texas State Penitentiary at Huntsville, Texas and was buried in Captain Joe Byrd Cemetery – aka Peckerwood Hill – in Huntsville, Texas. He lies in an unmarked grave after vandals repeatedly damaged or stole his tombstone.

DAVID BERKOWITZ: SON OF SAM

At 1am on 29 July 1976, 19-year-old Jody Valente and 18-year-old Donna Lauria were sitting in Jody's car outside Donna's home in the Bronx borough of New York. It was a hot summer night and they were discussing their boyfriends. Then Donna said goodnight and opened the door to get out.

A young man was standing a few feet away. He was holding a brown paper bag. As the car door opened, he reached into the bag, pulled out a gun and dropped into the crouching position.

'What does this guy want?' said Donna, rather alarmed.

Before the words were out of her mouth a bullet struck her in the side of the neck. A second bullet smashed the window in the door. A third smashed her elbow as she raised her hands to protect her face. Fatally wounded, she tumbled out of the car on to the sidewalk. The killer then shot Jody in the thigh. She fell forward on to the car's horn, which sounded and the killer made off.

Donna's father, Mike Lauria, was taking the family's dog for a walk and was halfway down the stairs when he heard the shots. He ran the rest of the way. Jody was still conscious, though hysterical. In the ambulance, Lauria begged his daughter not to die. It was too late. When Donna reached the hospital, she was pronounced DOA – dead on arrival. Jody was treated for hysteria, but nevertheless gave the police a good description of their assailant. He was a white male, about 30 years old, clean shaven with dark curly hair. He was not a rejected boyfriend. In fact, Jody had never seen him before. The only other clue to his identity was a yellow car parked near Jody's, which had gone by the time the police arrived. But New York is full of yellow cars.

The car in question actually belonged to David Berkowitz. In the days leading up to the murder, he had been looking for a job. But he had spent the nights, he said, 'looking for a victim, waiting for a signal'. Demon voices inside him told him to kill.

'I never thought I could kill her,' he said of Donna Lauria. 'I just fired the gun, you know, at the car, at the windshield. I never knew she was shot.'

The North Bronx, where the Laurias lived, was a mainly Italian area and the police immediately suspected Mafia involvement. However, the Mafia are usually scrupulous when it comes to contract killings. Women and children are out of bounds. Besides, ballistics tests showed that the murder weapon was a Charter Arms five-round .44 Bulldog revolver. It had a powerful recoil and was grossly inaccurate at distances of more than a few yards – hardly a hitman's weapon.

Lucky escape

On the other side of the East River from the Bronx lies the borough of Queens. It is a comfortable middle-class area. Eighteen-year-old student Rosemary Keenan attended Queens College there. Twelve weeks after the murder of Donna Lauria, she went to a bar in the Flushing area of Queens. There she met 20-year-old record salesman Carl Denaro, who was enjoying his last few days of freedom before joining the Air Force. Rosemary and Carl left together in Rosemary's red Volkswagen. They were parked up, talking, when a man crept up on them. He had a .44 Bulldog handgun tucked in his belt. He may have thought Carl, who was sitting in the passenger seat, was a woman because he had long brown hair. He pulled out his gun and fired five times through the passenger window. The shooting was wildly inaccurate and only one bullet found its mark. As Carl threw himself forward to protect himself from flying glass, it clipped the back of his head. It knocked away part of the skull but did not damage the brain. Carl Denaro was lucky. He did not die. After a two-month stay in hospital, he recovered completely. But the metal plate they put in his head ended his career in the Air Force before it had begun. Keenan had only superficial injuries from the shattered glass and drove off quickly before there were more shots.

On the evening of 27 November 1976, two schoolgirls, 16-year-old Donna DeMasi and her 18-year-old friend Joanne Lomino, were sitting on the front porch of Joanne's home on 262nd Street in Queens. At the end of the conversation, they said goodnight and Joanne stood up and reached in her handbag for her front door keys. It was then that the two girls noticed a man walking down the other side of the road. He was acting rather suspiciously. When he saw them, he suddenly changed direction. After crossing the street at the corner, he came over to them as if he was going to ask for directions. Instead, he pulled a gun from his waistband and began firing.

The two girls fled toward the front door, Joanne frantically searching for her keys. The first bullet hit her in the back. The second hit Donna in the neck. They stumbled into the bushes as the gunman loosed off the remaining three shots – all of which missed. He ran off down 262nd street and was spotted by a neighbour, gun still in hand.

The two wounded girls were rushed to Long Island Jewish Hospital, where Donna was found not to be badly injured. After three weeks, she made a full recovery. But Joanne was not so lucky. The bullet had smashed her spinal cord. She was paralysed from the waist down and would spend the rest of her life in a wheelchair. The neighbour who had spotted the gunman making his escape gave the police a description. One key feature he mentioned was the young man's dark curly hair. This was strange as the girls themselves claimed that he had long fair hair. Nevertheless, this tied the shooting of Donna DeMasi and Joanne Lomino to the man who had killed Donna Lauria and wounded Jody Valente.

On 29 January 1977, 30-year-old John Diel and his 26-year-old girlfriend, Christine Freund, had been to see the movie *Rocky* in Queens. Afterwards they went for dinner at the Wine Gallery in Austin Street, where they discussed their forthcoming engagement. Soon after midnight, the couple walked a few blocks to where their Pontiac Firebird was parked. It was cold outside and their breath fogged the windows. They were eager to get home but stopped for a moment and kissed. Then John turned the key in the ignition. But before he could pull away, he heard the blast of gunfire. The passenger window shattered and Christine slumped forward, bleeding. She died a few hours later in St John's Hospital of bullet wounds in the right temple and the neck. She had never even seen her killer. But he had seen her – so had the demons within him. Berkowitz later claimed that he had heard voices commanding him to 'get her, get her and kill her'. After firing three shots and realizing that he had hit her, he felt calm again.

'The voices stopped,' he said. 'I satisfied the demon's lust.'

More mayhem

After the murder of Christine Freund, Berkowitz completely gave in to the impulse to kill. After all, he was being rewarded with all the publicity he was getting. 'I had finally convinced myself that I was good to do it, and that the public wanted me to kill,' Berkowitz said later.

However, the New York Police Department were on his trail. Their ballistics lab ascertained that the bullet that had killed Christine Freund had also come from a .44 Bulldog handgun. That, in turn, tied it to the murder of Donna Lauria and the shootings of Jody Valente, Carl Denaro, Donna DeMasi and Joanne Lomino. However, apart from the mention of dark curly hair by Jody Valente and the neighbour in the DeMasi–Lomino case, the descriptions of the gunman varied so widely – if he'd been seen at all – that no one in the NYPD had yet concluded that the four shootings were the work of a single individual.

Six weeks later, on 8 March 1977, Virginia Voskerichian, a 19-year-old Armenian student, left Columbia University in Manhattan after her day's study and set off home to Forest Hills, Queens. Around 7.30pm, she was nearing her home on Exeter Street. A young man was approaching her on the sidewalk and she, politely, stepped out of his way. But he pulled a gun and shoved it in her face. She raised her books in a vain attempt to protect herself. He fired. The bullet tore through them. It entered through her upper lip, smashing out several teeth, and lodged in her brain. Virginia collapsed in the bushes at the side of the street and died instantly. A witness saw a young man running away and said he was about 18 and 5 ft 8 in tall. But there was no dark curly hair to be seen. The killer was wearing a balaclava.

He was almost caught that day. Minutes after the murder of Virginia Voskerichian, the police put out a 'Code .44'. Two police officers were assigned to the south end of the Bronx with orders to stop all cars containing a single white man. Berkowitz drove up to the checkpoint with his .44 Bulldog loaded and lying in plain view on the passenger seat of his Ford Galaxie. He was third in line when the police called off the search and he could not believe his luck when he watched the officers walk away.

It was quickly established that the bullet that killed Virginia Voskerichian was a .44 calibre. The riflings matched the marks on the bullet that had killed Christine Freund six weeks before and just a few miles away. Two days later, it was established that the same gun was responsible for the shooting of seven people.

On the afternoon of 10 March 1977, a press conference was held at One Police Plaza, the 13-storey red stone building that is New York's equivalent of London's New Scotland Yard. Police Commissioner Mike Codd stood with some trepidation before New York's hard-bitten crime reporters. As he read his carefully prepared statement, he began to have an inkling that he was unleashing a wave of hysteria that would engulf the city. He started by saying that the murder of Donna Lauria, nine months before, was linked to the killing of Virginia Voskerichian a mere two days before. In both cases, the killer had used a .44 Bulldog revolver. The same gun had also been used in three other incidents. Worse, the killer chose his victims completely at random. Reporters pushed for further information. Commissioner Codd said that the police were looking for a Caucasian male, about 6 ft tall, medium build, 25 to 30 years old, with dark hair. Next day, the '.44 Caliber Killer' made the headlines.

The man in charge of the investigation was Deputy Inspector Timothy J. Dowd of Omega task force set up to capture the .44 killer. Under him was Chief of Detectives John Keenan, who had a special reason for wanting to catch the killer. His daughter was the girl in the car with Carl Denaro when he was shot in the head.

'I know he was aiming for her,' Keenan said. 'So let's just say I put a little more than I had to into this case.'

Lunatic letter

The police realized that their chances of catching a lone, seemingly motiveless killer on the streets of New York were remote, so they asked for the help of every New Yorker. Tip-offs jammed the police switchboards. Dowd and his detectives had to follow up 250 to 300 leads a day.

However, Berkowitz took pity on the police. He wrote them a letter. But dropping it in a mailbox and letting the postal service deliver it was too mundane.

On the night of 16 April 1977, another young couple went to the movies in New York. They were 18-year-old Valentina Suriani and her boyfriend, 20-year-old Alexander Esau. After they had seen the film, they went on to a party. Around 3am, they were parked in a borrowed Mercury Montego outside Valentina's apartment building in the North Bronx, only three blocks from where Donna Lauria had been killed. Valentina was sitting on Alexander's lap with her legs stretched out across the passenger seat, enjoying a prolonged series of goodnight kisses when bullets shattered the passenger window. Two hit Valentina's head, killing her instantly. Another two hit Alexander Esau in the top of the head as he dived across the seat towards the passenger door. He died two hours later.

When the police arrived, they found a white envelope in the middle of the road by the car. It was addressed to Captain Joe Borelli, Deputy Inspector Dowd's second-in-command. The letter was all in capitals and full of spelling mistakes. It appeared to be the work of a madman. The writer claimed that he had been ordered to kill by his father, who was a vampire. His father's name, the writer said, was Sam – hence the new macabre sobriquet of the '.44 Caliber Killer', 'Son of Sam'. In the letter, he professed to love the people of Queens, but said he intended to kill more of them – particularly the women, which he spelt as if it rhymed with 'demon'. The writer signed off with the words:

'I SAY GOODBYE AND GOODNIGHT. POLICE: LET ME HAUNT YOU WITH THESE WORDS; I'LL BE BACK! I'LL BE BACK! TO BE INTERPRETED AS – BANG BANG, BANG, BANG, BANK, BANG – UGH!! YOURS IN MURDER, MR. MONSTER.'

By the time the letter reached the police labs, eight policemen had handled it. Only tiny traces of the writer's fingerprints remained. He appeared to have held the letter by the tips of his fingers and there was not enough of a print on the paper to identify the sender. Consequently, the police kept the existence of the letter secret. However, they showed a copy to celebrated New York columnist Jimmy Breslin. He dropped hints about the letter in his column in the *New York Daily News*.

On 1 June 1977, Breslin himself received a letter. It had been posted two days before in Englewood, New Jersey, just over the George Washington Bridge from Manhattan. The *Daily News*, then the biggest-selling newspaper in America, held back publication of the full letter for six days as speculation, and circulation, mounted. On 3 June 1977, the *News* ran the front-page headline: 'THE .44 CALIBER KILLER – NEW NOTE: CAN'T STOP KILLING'. The next day, they ran: '.44 KILLER: I AM NOT ASLEEP'. By Sunday, they were running: 'BRESLIN TO .44 KILLER: GIVE UP! IT'S THE ONLY WAY OUT'. This edition sold out within an hour of going on sale, so the presses kept rolling. By the end of the day, the paper had sold 1,116,000 copies – a record beaten only on the day Berkowitz was arrested. The editors assumed that interest had peaked and reproduced the letter in full in the Monday edition. Again, it was written all in capital letters and showed the same uncertain grasp of basic spelling. The letter was something of an anticlimax as it was as rambling and incoherent as the letter he had sent before to the police. It signed off:

'NOT KNOWING WHAT THE FUTURE HOLDS I SHALL SAY FAREWELL AND I WILL SEE YOU AT THE NEXT JOB, OR SHOULD I SAY YOU WILL SEE MY HANDIWORK AT THE NEXT JOB? REMEMBER MS. LAURIA. THANK YOU. IN THEIR BLOOD AND FROM THE GUTTER, "SAM'S CREATION". 44.'

Then there was a long postscript:

> 'HERE ARE SOME NAMES TO HELP YOU ALONG.
> FORWARD THEM TO THE INSPECTOR FOR USE BY THE
> NCIC: "THE DUKE OF DEATH". "THE WICKED KING
> WICKER", "THE TWENTY TWO DISCIPLES OF HELL",
> JOHN "WHEATIES" – RAPIST AND SUFFOCATER OF
> YOUNG GIRLS.
>   PS: J.B. PLEASE INFORM ALL THE DETECTIVES
> WORKING THE SLAYINGS TO REMAIN.'

At the police's request, this last page was withheld from publication. The reason they gave was that they did not want the NCIC – the National Crime Information Center – known about. But the .44 killer certainly knew about it. Perhaps the real reason was the satanic undertones in the list of pseudonyms he gives. The 'Wicked King Wicker' is presumably 'wicca'. The 'Twenty Two Disciples of Hell' sounds like some satanic organization. The name 'Wheaties' was put in inverted commas as if it were a nickname. John 'Wheaties' was supposed to be a 'rapist and suffocater of young girls'. The police could find no trace of him. In fact, none of the names were much help to the Omega team or the NCIC. Nor were they any use to Jimmy Breslin who now began calling the .44 killer the 'Son of Sam'.

Streets of fear

Seventeen-year-old Bronx schoolgirl Judy Placido went to the same school as Valentina Suriani and had been to her funeral. Three weeks after the Breslin letter appeared, on 25 June, she celebrated her graduation from high school at a discotheque in Queens called Elephas. There she met a handsome young man called Salvatore Lupo, who worked in a gas station. They hit it off immediately and went outside to a car for some privacy. As Salvatore slipped his arm around Judy's shoulders, they discussed the Son of Sam killings. At that moment, their lurid speculation turned into murderous reality. A .44 bullet smashed through the passenger window, passing through Salvatore's wrist and into Judy's neck. A second bullet hit her in the head, but miraculously failed to penetrate the skull. A third bullet entered her right shoulder. Terrified, Salvatore threw open the car door and ran back to the discotheque for help. But it was too late. The shooting was over and the attacker had fled.

Although she had been hit three times, Judy was quite unaware that she had been shot. She was shocked to see in the rear-view mirror that her face was covered with blood. She too jumped out of the car and headed for the disco, but she only made it a few yards before she collapsed. Salvatore suffered a shattered wrist and cuts from the flying glass. And in hospital, it was found that, unbelievably, Judy had escaped without serious injury.

Nevertheless, New York was in panic. Takings at discotheques and restaurants – particularly in Queens – plummeted, while newspaper circulations soared. Not only did they have the gory details of the latest shooting to relay, they could speculate about the next killing.

In the Son of Sam's letter to Jimmy Breslin, he had written: 'TELL ME JIM, WHAT WILL YOU HAVE FOR JULY TWENTY-NINTH?' That was the date of the first murder. Was he planning to celebrate the anniversary of the killing of Donna Lauria with another murder? New York's Mayor Abraham Beame could not wait to find out. He was running for re-election. He quickly announced that even more officers were being seconded to the investigation. Overnight, Omega became the largest single operation in the history of the New York Police Department. Two hundred men were on the case. They recruited from every borough of the city. The investigation cost more than $90,000 a day to run. Volunteers, such as Donna Lauria's father, Mike, manned special Son of Sam patrols and the hotline, which by then was receiving at least 5,000 calls a day. A team of psychiatrists tried to come up with some sort of profile of the killer. The best they could come up with was that he was 'neurotic, schizophrenic and paranoid'. This description was duly released by the police. It did not help anyone to identify the gunman.

Fortunately, 29 July 1977 passed without incident. But two days later, with a sense of relief, two sisters from Brooklyn, 15-year-old Ricki Moskowitz and 20-year-old Stacy, decided to go out. In a Brooklyn restaurant, they were approached by a handsome young man who introduced himself as Bobby Violante. The next day, Bobby and Stacy went to see the movie *New York, New York*. Afterwards, they went to dinner, then headed off to a quiet place where they could be alone. They drove to a secluded spot on Shore Parkway near Coney Island, South Brooklyn, which was used as an urban lovers' lane. They felt safe enough there. So far there had been no Son-of-Sam killings in the borough of Brooklyn. The nearest shooting had taken place 22 miles away in Queens. What they did not know was that, a week before, a man claiming to be the Son of Sam had phoned the Coney Island precinct and said that he would strike next in that area. Extra patrol cars were assigned to Brooklyn and Coney Island. Shore Parkway was being patrolled regularly.

Bobby Violante and Stacy Moskowitz pulled up under a street lamp, the only available parking spot. There was a full moon that night. It was not dark enough for what they had in mind, so the two of them went for a walk in the park nearby. They walked over a bridge and spent a few minutes playing on the swings. Near the public toilets, they noticed a man in jeans, who they described as a 'hippie type', leaning against a wall. He was not there when they walked back to the car. Back in the car, they kissed. Stacy suggested that they move on, but Bobby wanted one more kiss. It was a mistake.

While they were embracing, Bobby Violante took two bullets in the face, blinding him and exploding his eardrums. He could neither see nor hear, but he felt Stacy jerk violently in his arms, then collapse forward. He feared she was dead. Bobby threw himself against the car horn, fumbled at the car door, cried for help, then collapsed on the pavement.

In the car in front, Tommy Zaino had seen the shooting in his rear-view mirror. He had watched as a man approached the car from behind and pulled out a gun. From a crouching position, he had fired four shots through the open passenger window. When his girlfriend, Debbie Crescendo, heard the shooting, she said: 'What's that?'

Zaino thought he knew.

'Get down,' he said. 'I think it's the Son of Sam.'

Zaino watched as the gunman ran towards the park. He looked at his watch. It was exactly 2.35am. A patrol car was just five blocks away at the time.

Stacy Moskowitz was still conscious when the ambulance arrived. One bullet had grazed her scalp, but the other had lodged in the back of her brain. She died 38 hours later. Bobby Violante survived, but his sight could not be restored.

Tommy Zaino gave a good description of the killer. He was stocky with stringy, fair hair. This matched the description given by Donna DeMasi and Joanne Lomino, but not the dark, curly-haired man described by Jody Valente and the neighbour in the DeMasi–Lomino case. The police wondered whether he was wearing a wig.

A beautician and her boyfriend were seated by the entrance to the park when they heard the shots. They saw a man wearing a denim jacket and what they took to be a cheap nylon wig. He jumped into a light-coloured car and drove off, as if he had just robbed a bank. A young girl on a bicycle identified the car as a yellow Volkswagen. A nurse, who looked out of the window when she heard the shots, also said that she had seen a yellow VW. It almost collided with another car at the first intersection and the driver was so incensed that he gave chase, only to lose the car after a couple of blocks. The yellow VW's driver, he said, had stringy brown hair.

New evidence

But an even more vital witness took a little longer to come forward. She was Mrs Cacilia Davis, a 49-year-old widow, who had been out with a male friend. They had returned to her apartment, two blocks from the park, at around 2am. They sat and talked for a few minutes, but as they had been forced to double park, they kept an eye open for other cars. A little way ahead, Mrs Davis saw a police car and two patrolmen writing out parking tickets. Some way behind was a yellow Ford Galaxie. It was parked by a fire hydrant and, a few minutes before, an officer from the patrol car had given it a ticket. A young man with dark hair walked up to the Galaxie and irritably pulled the parking ticket from the windscreen.

David Berkowitz.

Mrs Davis invited her friend in for coffee. He declined, saying that it was 2.20am already. At that moment, the police car pulled off. So did the Galaxie, but it could not get past Mrs Davis's friend's car. The man in the Galaxie impatiently honked the horn. Mrs Davis hurriedly got out and her friend pulled off. The Galaxie followed, passing him quickly and speeding after the police car. Minutes later, Mrs Davis went out to take her dog for a walk in the park. She noticed Tommy Zaino's car, Bobby Violante's car and a VW van. On her way home, she saw a man with dark hair and a blue denim jacket striding across the road from the cars. He glared at her and he was walking with his right arm stiff, as if something was concealed up his sleeve. He also looked rather like the man with the Ford Galaxie she had seen earlier.

Mrs Davis did not come forward with this information immediately, though. She realized that, if the man she had seen was the Son of Sam, she was in danger. He could easily identify her and he knew where she lived. Two days after the shooting, Mrs Davis told two close friends what she had seen. They realized that she might have a vital clue and urged her to call the police. Eventually, her friends called the police on her behalf. Detective Joseph Strano visited her and took her statement. It caused hardly a ripple. Tommy Zaino was considered the best witness to the shooting. He had seen a man with fair hair, not dark. And the driver of the Ford Galaxie had left the scene of the crime before the shooting.

But Mrs Davis now felt that she had risked her life to come forward and would not be ignored. She threatened to go, anonymously, to the newspapers with her story. To humour her, Detective Strano interviewed her again, bringing along a police artist to make a sketch of the man. He also took her on a shopping expedition to see if she could pick out a similar denim jacket. But still nothing got done. The problem with her story was that the local police had not issued any parking tickets in that area that night. But the police cars patrolling the area had been seconded from other boroughs.

It was ten days before four missing tickets turned up. Three of the cars were quickly eliminated. The fourth, a yellow Galaxie, number 561-XLB, belonged to a David Berkowitz of 35 Pine Street, Yonkers, a suburban area just north of the Bronx. Detective James Justus called Yonkers police headquarters. Switchboard operator Wheat Carr answered. Justus said that he was working on the Son-of-Sam case and that he was checking on David Berkowitz. The woman shouted: 'Oh, no.'

Not only did she know David Berkowitz, but she had also suspected that he was the Son of Sam for some time.

Her suspicions had begun the previous year when her father began to receive anonymous letters complaining about his dog. In October, a petrol bomb had been thrown through the window of the Carrs' house at 316 Warburton Avenue, Yonkers. A neighbour had also been receiving anonymous letters and abusive phone calls. On Christmas Eve 1976, someone had fired a number of shots through their window and killed their Alsatian. Then, on 27 April 1977, someone entered the Carrs' backyard and shot their black Labrador, Harvey. On 10 June 1977, Wheat's father, Sam Carr, had received a phone call from a man named Jack Cassaras who lived in New Rochelle, out on Long Island Sound. Mr Cassaras wanted to know why Mr Carr had sent him a get-well card. The card said that Mr Cassaras had fallen off a roof. He had not, nor had he ever, been on one. Mr Carr had no explanation and invited Mr Cassaras over to discuss the matter. The drive took about 20 minutes. Sam Carr examined the card. Strangely, it had a picture of an Alsatian on it and Mr Carr told Cassaras about the bizarre things that had been happening. Mr Cassaras drove home even more puzzled, but his son thought that he had the answer.

The year before, the Cassaras family had rented out a room above their garage to a David Berkowitz. He had complained about the

Cassarases' Alsatian. After a few weeks, he had left suddenly without collecting the deposit of $200. When Mrs Cassaras looked David Berkowitz up in the telephone directory, she found that he now lived at 35 Pine Street, Yonkers. She rang Sam Carr and asked him whether Pine Street was near them. It was right around the corner. Mr Carr then became convinced that David Berkowitz was responsible for the harassment they had suffered and went to the police. However, the police explained that they could take the matter no further without more concrete evidence.

The breakthrough

Another of Berkowitz's neighbours, Craig Glassman, had also been receiving abusive letters. He lived in the apartment underneath Berkowitz. But he was a police officer and when, a week after the Moskowitz murder, rubbish was piled against Glassman's front door and set on fire, he reported it. That was 6 August 1977. He also showed detectives two anonymous letters he had received. They accused Glassman of being a spy planted there by Sam Carr. Glassman and the Carrs were part of a black-magic sect out to get him, the author alleged. The detective who examined the letters recognized the handwriting. It belonged to another man he was investigating – David Berkowitz.

However, Berkowitz was not the only suspect in the Son-of-Sam slayings. New York has a rich supply of potential serial killers. Besides, Berkowitz did not fit the description given by Tommy Zaino. Nor did he drive a yellow VW, so it was not until 10 August 1977 that detectives John Longo and Ed Zigo went to Yonkers to check Berkowitz out. Zigo spotted Berkowitz's Ford Galaxie parked outside the apartment block in Pine Street. There was a bag on the back seat with a rifle butt protruding from it. In New York back then, possessing a rifle did not even require a licence. Nevertheless, Zigo forced open the car. Inside, he found another, more formidable weapon, a Commando Mark III semi-automatic. Then in the glove compartment, he found a letter addressed to Deputy Inspector Timothy Dowd, head of the Son of Sam investigation. It said that the next shooting would be in Long Island. Detective Zigo phoned in and told Sergeant James Shea: 'I think we've got him.'

Police from all over the city were brought in. They staked out the car for six hours until Berkowitz turned up. He was a stocky man with a round cherubic face and dark hair. When he got into the driver's seat, he found himself staring down the barrel of a police revolver.

'Freeze!' yelled Detective William Gardella. 'Police!'

Berkowitz simply smiled.

Detective John Falotico opened the passenger door, held his .38 to Berkowitz's head and told him to get out. When he put his hands on the roof, Falotico asked: 'Who are you?'

Berkowitz answered: 'I am Sam.'

At One Police Plaza, Berkowitz confessed to the shootings and the anonymous letters. He also admitted that his crime spree had begun on Christmas Eve 1975. About seven o'clock, he drove to Co-op City in the Bronx, where his adoptive father lived. He saw a young Hispanic woman leaving a store and followed her. He pulled a knife and stabbed her in the back. She did not realize what had happened, turned, screamed and grabbed his wrist. He ran away. But on his way home, he followed 15-year-old Michelle Forman and stabbed her in the back and head. She fell screaming on the sidewalk. Again, Berkowitz fled. Somehow, she managed to stagger to the apartment block where her parents lived. They rushed her to hospital where they found that she had a collapsed lung. Her other injuries were superficial and she only spent a week in hospital. His first victim did not even report the attack and was never identified. These early attacks convinced Berkowitz that he needed a gun. A friend called Billy Dan Parka bought him a .44 Bulldog revolver in Houston, Texas for $130. Under interrogation,

Berkowitz explained that he had been ordered to commit the murders by Sam Carr, via Carr's demon dog Harvey. Other demon voices accompanied him when he was stalking his victims. Berkowitz was so forthcoming that his complete confession took only half an hour.

Further enquiries revealed that Richard David Berkowitz had been an illegitimate child who had been given up for adoption as a baby. His natural mother, Betty Broder, was Jewish. At 19, she married Tony Falco, an Italian-American. He left her for another woman six years later. She began an affair with real estate agent Joseph Kleinman, a married man, in 1947. She got pregnant by him, but when she told him that she was going to have a child, he said she had better get rid of it if she wanted to go on seeing him. The child was born on 1 June 1953 and was adopted immediately by a Jewish couple, Pearl and Nathan Berkowitz, who were unable to have children of their own. They named him David. But in 1967, when David was just 14, Pearl Berkowitz succumbed to cancer. He was deeply upset at this new loss.

Two years later, Nathan decided to move to Co-op City in the Bronx, a middle-class suburb. But the area was on the skids and gangs of youths soon began terrorizing the neighbourhood. David's school grades plunged and he seemed to lose any sense of direction. He was shy and found himself a victim of bullying, though others saw him as spoilt and something of a bully himself. He was big for his age, strong and an excellent baseball player. But he liked to play with kids younger than himself. His biggest problem was with girls. One friend remembers Berkowitz asking him if he wanted to join the 'girl-haters' club'. He only ever dated one girl in Co-op City, Iris Gerhardt. She liked his warm and obliging nature, but the relationship was never consummated. While Berkowitz remained chaste, almost everyone else seemed to be at it.

'After a while, at Co-op City, there wasn't one girl who was a virgin,' he said resentfully.

Later, in prison, Berkowitz wrote: 'I must slay women for revenge purposes to get back at them for all the suffering they caused me.'

His friends also started smoking marijuana, but, again, Berkowitz was too inhibited to join in. Things got worse in 1971 when his foster father remarried. Berkowitz resented his stepmother and stepsister, and decided to join the army. But that did not last long. Home again in 1974, Berkowitz had rejected Judaism and become a Baptist. Nathan Berkowitz remembered his son standing in front of the mirror beating his head with his fists. Things became so uncomfortable in the Berkowitz household that David moved out to take a drab one-room apartment at 2151 Barnes Avenue in the Bronx. By this time, Nathan became convinced that his son needed psychiatric help. But Nathan and his new family were moving to Florida and nothing was done. With his foster father gone, another door closed for Berkowitz.

He had known that he had been adopted from the age of seven. Isolated, he tried to trace his real family. It took a year. Through the Bureau of Records, he discovered that his real name was Richard Falco and he came from Brooklyn. Using an old telephone directory, he managed to trace his mother and an older sister. He dropped a card in his mother's mailbox and, a few days later, she called him. The reunion was emotional. He also met his 37-year-old sister and became a regular visitor to the house where she lived with her husband and children. At last, he had found a family and, at last, Berkowitz was happy. Or so it seemed.

In the first half of 1976, his visits to his real mother and sister became increasingly rare. He complained of headaches. In February, he moved into the room above the Cassarases' garage out in New Rochelle. Two months later, he moved suddenly to Pine Street, Yonkers. In July, he killed Donna Lauria.

After a year-long killing spree the police at last had Berkowitz under lock and key. Judged sane enough to stand trial, Berkowitz pleaded guilty to all charges and was given six life sentences. Sergeant Joseph Coffey, who had conducted the initial interrogation, said: 'I feel sorry for him. The man is a fucking vegetable.'

However, not everyone was satisfied with Berkowitz's conviction. Young Yonkers-born investigative journalist, Maury Terry, spotted a number of inconsistencies in Berkowitz's story.

Berkowitz claimed that he had acted alone, but descriptions of the killer varied wildly. Terry also noted that some of the Son-of-Sam killings had been performed with a ruthless efficiency. Others were inept and bungled. Terry concluded that Berkowitz had only committed three of the Son-of-Sam killings – those of Donna Lauria, Valentina Suriani and Alexander Esau.

Terry believes that Berkowitz was a member of a satanic organization – 'The Twenty Two Disciples of Hell' – and that other members of the cult were responsible for the other killings. The killer in the balaclava, Terry believes, was actually a woman member. However, when he tracked down other members – who included Sam Carr's two sons, John 'Wheaties' and Michael – they had all died mysteriously before he caught up with them.

In February 1979, Berkowitz issued a statement from Attica Correctional Facility, saying that he was indeed involved with a satanic group. Then on 10 July 1979, he was slashed with a razor by another inmate. The cut ran from the left-hand side of his throat to the back of his neck. It needed 56 stitches and nearly killed him. Berkowitz insisted that the attack was a warning from his satanic group to make him shut up.

DENNIS NILSEN: KILLING FOR COMPANY

Of Dennis Nilsen's 15 victims, only one – a Canadian tourist – was missed. The rest were homosexual drifters who were looking for money, or love, or just a place to stay the night. Instead, they were killed to become the companion and sexual plaything of a prolific serial killer.

Nilsen was born in Fraserburgh, a small town on the bleak northeast coast of Scotland, on 23 November 1945. His father was a Norwegian soldier, who had escaped to Scotland after the German invasion of Norway in 1940 and had married Betty Whyte, a local girl, in 1942. The marriage did not work out and Betty continued to live with her parents. After a few years, the couple divorced.

Dennis grew up with his mother, elder brother and younger sister, but the strongest influence on his young life were his stern and pious grandparents. Their faith was so strict that they banned alcohol from the house. The radio and cinema were considered the instruments of the devil. Nilsen's grandmother would not even cook on the Lord's day and their Sunday lunch had to be prepared the day before.

The young Nilsen was sullen and intensely withdrawn. The only person who could penetrate his private world was his grandfather, Andrew Whyte. A fisherman, he was Nilsen's hero. He would regale the little boy with tales of the sea and his ancestors lost beneath its churning waves.

When Andrew Whyte died of a heart attack at sea in 1951, his body was brought home and laid out on the dining room table. Dennis was invited to come and view his grandad, so, at the age of six, he got his first glimpse of a corpse. From that moment, the images of death and love fused in his mind.

He left school at 15 and went into the army. After basic training, he joined the catering corps. There he was taught how to sharpen knives – and how to dissect a carcass. During his life in the army, Nilsen only had one close friend. He persuaded him to pose for photographs, sprawled on the ground as if he had been killed in battle.

One night in Aden, Nilsen was drunk and fell asleep in the back of a cab. He woke to find himself naked, locked in the boot. When the cab driver returned, Nilsen played dead. Then as he was man-handled out of the boot, Nilsen grabbed a jack handle and beat him around the head. Nilsen never knew whether he had killed the man. After that, he began having nightmares of being raped, tortured and mutilated.

After 11 years in the army, Nilsen left to join the police force instead. Part of his training included a visit to a mortuary. The partially dissected corpses fascinated Nilsen. He did well in the police, but his private life was gradually disintegrating. Death became an obsession. He liked to masturbate while pretending to be a corpse, lying naked in front of a mirror with blue paint smeared on his lips and his skin whitened with talcum powder.

His incipient homosexuality began to bother him. After 11 months in the police force, he caught two men committing an act of gross indecency in a parked car. He could not bring himself to arrest them and decided to resign.

Too drunk to have sex

He went to work interviewing applicants at the Jobcentre in London's Charing Cross Road, where he became branch secretary of the civil service union and developed increasingly radical political views. Nevertheless, his work was good enough to earn him promotion to executive officer at the Jobcentre in Kentish Town, north London.

Despite his professional progress, Nilsen was lonely and yearned for a lasting relationship. Since his teens, he had been aware of his attraction towards other men, but in the army and in the police force he had somehow managed to repress it. In 1975, he met a young man called David Gallichen outside a pub. They moved into a flat at 195 Melrose Avenue, Cricklewood, together, with a cat and a dog called Bleep. Gallichen, or Twinkle as Nilsen called him, stayed at home and decorated the flat, while Nilsen went to work. They made home movies together and spent a lot of time drinking and talking. But the relationship did not last. And when Gallichen moved out, Nilsen was plunged back into a life of loneliness.

On New Year's Eve 1978, Nilsen met a teenage Irish boy in a pub and invited him back to Melrose Avenue. They were too drunk to have sex. When Nilsen woke in the morning, the boy was lying fast asleep beside him. He was afraid that, when the boy woke up, he would leave – and Nilsen wanted him to stay.

Their clothes were thrown together in a heap on the floor. Nilsen leant over and grabbed his tie. Then he put the tie around the boy's neck and pulled. The boy woke immediately and began to struggle. They rolled on to the floor, but Nilsen kept pulling on the tie.

After about a minute, the boy's body went limp, but he was still breathing. Nilsen went to the kitchen and filled a bucket with water.

He brought the bucket back and held the boy's head underwater until he drowned. Now he had to stay.

Nilsen carried the dead boy into the bathroom and gave him a bath. He dried the corpse lovingly, then dressed it in clean socks and underpants. For a while, he just lay in bed holding the dead boy, then he put him on the floor and he went to sleep.

The following day, he planned to hide the body under the floor, but *rigor mortis* had stiffened the joints, making it hard to handle, so he left the body out while he went to work. When the corpse had loosened up, Nilsen undressed it again and washed it. This time he masturbated beside it. He found he could not stop playing with the boy's body and admiring it.

All the time Nilsen was playing with the corpse, he expected to be arrested at any moment. But no one came. It seemed no one had missed the dead boy. After a week living happily with the corpse, Nilsen hid it under the floorboards. Seven months later, he cut it up and burnt it in the back garden.

Disturbing feelings

Nilsen's first experience of murder frightened him. He was determined it would not happen again and decided to give up drinking. But Nilsen was lonely. He liked to go to pubs to meet people. Soon he slipped off the wagon.

Nearly a year later, on 3 December 1979, Nilsen met Kenneth Ockenden, a Canadian tourist, in a pub in Soho. Nilsen took the afternoon off work and joined Ockenden on a sight-seeing tour of London. Ockenden agreed to go back to Nilsen's flat for something to eat. After a visit to the off-licence, they sat in front of the television eating ham, eggs and chips and drinking beer, whisky and rum.

As the evening wore on, disturbing feelings began to grow inside Nilsen. He liked Ockenden, but realized that he would soon be leaving and going back to Canada. A feeling of desolation swept over him. It was the same feeling he had had when he killed the Irish boy.

Late that night, when they were both very drunk, Ockenden was listening to music through earphones. Nilsen put the flex of the earphones around Ockenden's neck and dragged him struggling across the floor. When he was dead, Nilsen took the earphones off and put them on himself. He poured himself another drink and listened to records.

In the early hours, he stripped the corpse and carried it over his shoulder into the bathroom. When the body was clean and dry, he put it on the bed and went to sleep next to it.

In the morning, he put the body in a cupboard and went to work. That evening, he took the body out and dressed it in clean socks, underpants and vest. He took some photographs of it, then laid it next to him on the bed. For the next two weeks, Nilsen would watch TV in the evening with Ockenden's body propped up in an armchair next to him. Last thing at night, he would undress it, wrap it in the curtains and place the body back under the floorboards.

Ockenden had gone missing from a hotel and his disappearance made the news for a few days. Again, Nilsen was convinced that he was about to be arrested at any moment. People in the pub, on the tour bus and in the local off-licence had seen them together. But still there was no knock at the door. From then on, Nilsen felt that he could pursue his gruesome hobby unfettered.

Obsession with bodies

Nilsen began to deliberately seek out victims. He would go to pubs where lonely young homosexuals hung out. He would buy them drinks, offer advice and invite them back to his flat for something to eat. Many accepted.

One of them was Martin Duffey. After a disturbed childhood, he had run away from home and ended up in London, sleeping in railway stations. He went back to Nilsen's and, after two cans of beer, crawled into bed. When he was asleep, Nilsen strangled him. Then he dragged Duffey's unconscious body into the kitchen, filled the sink and held his head underwater for four minutes.

Nilsen went through the standard procedure of stripping and bathing the corpse, then he took it to bed. He talked to it, complimenting Duffey on his body. He kissed it all over and masturbated over it. Nilsen kept the body in a cupboard for a few days. When it started to swell up, he put it under the floorboards.

Twenty-seven-year-old Billy Sutherland died because he was a nuisance. Nilsen didn't fancy him, but after meeting him on a pub crawl Sutherland followed him home. Nilsen vaguely remembered strangling him. There was certainly a dead body in the flat in the morning.

Nilsen did not even know some of his victims by name. He was not much interested in them – only their bodies, their dead bodies. The seductions and murders were sad and mechanical. But once the victims were dead, they really turned him on. Just touching the corpse would give him an erection.

Nilsen would go out to work perfectly normally. Then, when he got home in the evening, he would get his latest corpse out and play with it. It was a thrill to own a beautiful body. He would hold the corpse in a passionate embrace and talk to it, and when he was finished with it, he would stuff it under the floorboards.

Some of his murders were terrifyingly casual. Nilsen found one victim, a 24-year-old, Malcolm Barlow, collapsed on the pavement in Melrose Avenue. Barlow was an epileptic and said that the pills he was taking made his legs give way. Nilsen carried him home and called an ambulance. When he was released from hospital the next day, Barlow returned to Nilsen's flat. Nilsen prepared a meal. Barlow began drinking, even though Nilsen warned him not to mix alcohol with the new pills he had been prescribed. When Barlow collapsed, Nilsen could not be bothered to call the ambulance again and strangled him, then carried on drinking until bedtime. By now the space under the floorboards was full of corpses, so the next morning Nilsen stuffed Barlow's body in the cupboard under the sink.

As the place filled up, Nilsen decided it was time to move. There were six corpses under the floor, and several others had been dissected and stored in suitcases. He decided that he had better dispose of the bodies first. After a stiff drink, Nilsen pulled up the floorboards and began cutting up the corpses. He left the internal organs out in the garden. Birds and rats did the rest. The other body parts were wrapped in carpet and thrown on a bonfire with a car tyre on top to disguise the smell.

Breaking the cycle

Nilsen moved to an attic flat at 23 Cranley Gardens, Muswell Hill. This was a deliberate attempt to stop his murderous career. He could not kill people, he thought, if he had no floorboards to hide them under and no garden to burn them in. He had several casual encounters at his new flat, picking men up at night and letting them go in the morning, unmolested. This made him feel elated. He had finally broken the cycle.

But then John Howlett, or Guardsman John as Nilsen called him, came back to Cranley Gardens and Nilsen could not help himself. He strangled Howlett with a strap and drowned him. A few days later, he strangled Graham Allen while he was eating an omelette.

The death of his final victim, Stephen Sinclair, upset Nilsen. Sinclair was a drifter and a drug addict. When they met, Nilsen felt sorry for him and bought him a hamburger. Back at Cranley Gardens, he slumped in a chair in a stupor and Nilsen decided to relieve him of the pain of his miserable life. He got a piece of string from the kitchen, but it was not long enough. Then he got his one and only remaining tie and choked the life out of his unconscious victim.

Police escort a coffin from Nilsen's house.

Killing in Cranley Gardens presented Nilsen with a problem. He was forced to dispose of the bodies by dissecting them, boiling the flesh from the bones, dicing up the remains and flushing them down the toilet. Unfortunately, the drains in Muswell Hill were not built to handle bodies.

The drains at 23 Cranley Gardens had been blocked for five days on 8 February 1983, when Dyno-rod sent Michael Cattran to investigate. He quickly determined that the problem was not inside, but outside the house. At the side of the house, he found the manhole that led to the sewers. He removed the cover and climbed in.

At the bottom of the access shaft, he found a glutinous grey sludge. The smell was awful. As he examined it, more sludge came out of the pipe that led from the house. He called his manager and told him that he thought the substance he had found was human flesh.

Next morning, Cattran and his boss returned to the manhole, but the sludge had vanished. No amount of rainfall could have flushed it through. Someone had been down there and removed it.

Cattran put his hand inside the pipe that connected to the house and pulled out some more meat and four small bones. One of the tenants in the house said that they had heard footsteps on the stairs in the night and suspected that the man who lived in the attic flat had been down to the manhole. The police were called.

'I've come about the drains'

Detective Chief Inspector Peter Jay took the flesh and bones to Charing Cross Hospital. A pathologist there confirmed that the flesh was, indeed, human.

The tenant of the attic flat was out at work when Jay got back to Cranley Gardens. At 5.40pm that day, Nilsen returned. Inspector Jay met him at the front door and introduced himself. He said he had come about the drains. Nilsen remarked that it was odd that the police should be interested in drains.

Inside Nilsen's flat, Jay explained that the drains contained human remains.

'Good grief! How awful,' Nilsen exclaimed.

Jay told him to stop messing about.

'Where's the rest of the body?' Jay asked.

After a short pause, Nilsen said: 'In two plastic bags in the wardrobe next door. I'll show you.'

He showed Inspector Jay the wardrobe. The smell coming from it confirmed what he was saying.

'I'll tell you everything,' Nilsen said. 'I want to get it off my chest, not here but at the police station.'

The police could scarcely believe their ears when Nilsen admitted killing 15 or 16 men. But in the wardrobe in Nilsen's flat, they found two large black bin-liners. In one, they found a shopping bag containing the left side of a man's chest, including the arm. A second bag contained the right side of a chest and arm. In a third, there was a torso with no arms, legs or head. A fourth was full of human offal. The unbearable stench indicated that the bags had evidently been closed for some time.

In the second bin-liner, there were two heads – one with the flesh boiled away, the other largely intact – and another torso. The arms were still attached, but the hands were missing. One of the heads belonged to Stephen Sinclair. Nilsen had severed it only four days earlier and had started simmering it in a pot on the kitchen stove.

Under a drawer in the bathroom, the police found Sinclair's pelvis and legs. In a tea chest in Nilsen's bedroom, there was another torso, a skull and more bones.

The police also examined the gardens at 195 Melrose Avenue. They found human ash and enough fragments of bone to determine that at least eight people, probably more, had been cremated there. With Nilsen under arrest, intended victims who had escaped came forward.

Nilsen was eventually charged with six counts of murder and three of attempted murder. His solicitor had one simple question for Nilsen: 'Why?'

'I'm hoping you will tell me that,' Nilsen said.

Nilsen intended to plead guilty, sparing the jury and the victims' families the details of the horrendous crimes. Instead, his solicitor persuaded him to claim 'diminished responsibility'. He was sentenced to life imprisonment with the recommendation that he serve at least 25 years. He had served 35 when he died in 2018, aged 72.

DENNIS RADER: BTK

Although he appeared to be a normal, God-fearing American from a normal, God-fearing American family, Dennis Rader called himself BTK – standing for 'Bind them, Torture them, Kill them' – in letters he sent to the newspapers taunting the police for their inability to catch him. Despite this, he got away with killing ten people between 1974 and 1979. Then he stopped. It was only when he resumed writing letters in 2004 that he got caught.

Rader was born in Pittsburg, Kansas in 1945, after his father returned from serving in the Marine Corps during World War II. He was the first of four boys. When he was still a child, the family moved to Park City, a town just outside Wichita.

From the age of eight, Rader grew obsessed with the true crime and detective magazines of the era, with names such as *True Detective*, *Revealing Detective*, *Master Detective*, *Front Page*, *Climax*, *Vintage Sensation*, etc., that his father hid in his car. The stories were accompanied by photographs and artworks intended to titillate the male readership. In them, women were often hunted, tied up, tortured and killed. A solitary boy, Rader practised these techniques on animals and continued doing so until he enlisted in the US Air Force, aged 21.

His mother was a strict disciplinarian. She would beat her children, giving Rader the first inklings of sexual stimulation. This led him to masturbate while torturing small animals.

At school, he supplemented this with drawing women being subjugated and murdered. He would cut pictures of women out of magazines and underwear catalogues, adding gags, chains and ligatures around their necks. He earned a badge for knot-tying in the Boy Scouts.

From the age of 14, he became a peeping Tom and stalker, and would also break into homes in the neighbourhood to steal women's underwear. In his parents' basement, he would rig up ropes, pulleys and other bondage paraphernalia. Then he would photograph himself naked or in stolen women's clothes while restrained.

He enjoyed the military discipline of the Air Force, studied electronics and was posted to the Far East. In Japan, he visited brothels where he studied the finer points of bondage, domination, submission and autoeroticism. After four years in the service, he was honourably discharged and returned to Park City as well as to the old practices of photographing himself wearing women's clothes and make-up, or a mask, in bondage.

On the prowl

Meanwhile, he married, became the father of two children and took a job in the meat department of a supermarket where his mother worked. In the evenings and weekends, he studied criminal justice, with an emphasis on law enforcement, graduating with a bachelor's degree. He tried to join the police, but failed on psychological evaluation. However, he did work as a reserve police officer in a number of jurisdictions around the Wichita area. And he took a job in a security company, installing burglar alarms. This gave him a good knowledge of the districts and the homes where he would commit his murders.

He began picking people he would target for bondage, torture and killing. He would also build a number of 'hit kits', containing guns, knives, cords from Venetian blinds, black electrical tape, screwdrivers, wire-cutters, plastic bags, handcuffs and gloves. These would be carried in a small bag, attaché case or just stuffed in his pockets.

He came up with detailed plans for future crimes. These were known as projects. The murder of Vicki Wegerle was known as Project Piano since she played the piano, while Project Fox Hunt referred to the murder of Nancy Fox. These would join his ever-growing collection of autoerotic photographs and pictures showing men, women and children in bonds. As his murderous career got under way, he would also add press cuttings of his crimes, copies of letters and poems he sent about the crimes, and, eventually, books about the BTK killer, to his mother lode, all neatly filed in ten three-ring binders. As time went on, computer disks were added.

While these files swelled, he worked for the US Census Department as a city compliance officer, equipped with a badge, a gun, a citation book and authorization to prowl the streets at night. He was also elected to two city policy boards and the assembly of the Christ Lutheran Church in Wichita, where he rose to become vice-president.

His first murder took place in January 1974, when he killed four members of the Otero family in Wichita – 38-year-old Joseph Otero, his 33-year-old wife Julie, both from Puerto Rico, their 11-year-old daughter Josephine and nine-year-old son Joseph Jnr. Their bodies were found by their three older children, who had been at school.

'My dad's tongue was halfway bit off. He had a belt around his neck,' said Charlie Otero, who was 15 at the time. 'My mom was beaten, her nails were busted up. They were cold. We tried to get the ligatures undone, the belt undone and then I realized this was for nothing and that I had to get my brother and my sister out of the house.'

Rader had been lurking outside their home at 8.30am. Ten minutes later, the door opened as Joseph Jnr stepped out. Rader grabbed him and pushed him back inside. He threatened the family with a knife and gun, reassuring them that it was only a robbery. In fact, little Josephine was his target. Rader made her and Joseph watch as he killed their parents in their bedroom.

He then dragged Joseph to his bedroom and wrapped two T-shirts around his head and covered it with a plastic bag. Pulling up a chair, he watched as the boy struggled as he suffocated to death. Then he put a noose around the neck of the barely conscious Josephine and led her down to the basement.

Rader asked her if she had a camera as he wanted to take a picture. She didn't. Tying the noose over the sewer pipe, he pulled her clothes off and toyed with her.

'What's going to happen to me?' she asked. He said she would soon be in heaven with the others. Then he placed a gag in her mouth and hoisted her off the floor. As she writhed, Rader masturbated.

Asked if he ever wore a mask to disguise his identity, Rader said: 'No, because they weren't going to be alive when I left.'

The monster in the dark

Rader wrote a letter detailing the murders, which he left inside the book *Applied Engineering Mechanics* in Wichita Public Library in October 1974. On 22 October, he called Don Granger of the *Wichita Eagle* and *Beacon* newspapers telling them it was there. Granger retrieved the letter. Its authenticity was not in doubt as it contained details only the police and the killer could have known. It said that the three individuals being questioned for the Otero murders were not involved.

It was addressed to the 'Secret Witness Progam', where informants could pass on information to the police anonymously via the newspaper. The police asked the paper not to publish the contents of the letter to prevent them from having to deal with a spate of false confessions.

However, a reporter for a new rival newspaper called the *Wichita Sun* received a copy of the letter and printed part of it in an article on 11 December 1974. It said:

'I write this letter to you for the sake of the tax payer as well as your time. Those three dude you have in custody are just talking to get publicity for the Otero murders. They know nothing at all. I did it by myself and with no ones help. There has been no talk either. Let's put this straight ...' [The killer provides details of the crimes and crime scene that were not published in the paper.]

'I'm sorry this happen to society. They are the ones who suffer the most. It hard to control myself. You probably call me "psychotic with sexual perversion hang-up." When this monster enter my brain I will never know. But, it here to stay. How does one cure himself? If you ask for help, that you have killed four people they will laugh or hit the panic button and call the cops.

'I can't stop it so the monster goes on, and hurt me as well as society. Society can be thankful that there are ways for people like me to relieve myself at time by day dreams of some victims being torture and being mine. It a big complicated game my friend of the monster play putting victims number down, follow them, checking up on them, waiting in the dark, waiting, waiting ... the pressure is great and sometimes he run the game to his liking. Maybe you can stop him. I can't. He has already chosen his next victim or victims. I don't know who they are yet. The next day after I read the paper, I will know, but it to late. Good luck hunting.

'YOURS, TRULY GUILTILY'

Although the letter was unsigned, it contained a postscript which gave him his famous tag:

> 'P.S. Since sex criminals do not change their M.O. or by nature cannot do so, I will not change mine. The code word for me will be ... Bind them, torture them, kill them, B.T.K., you see me at it again. They will be on the next victim.'

Before the letter had been delivered, on 4 April 1974 he murdered 21-year-old Kathryn Bright in Operation Lights Out. He had decided that it would be easier to kill a woman who did not have any male family members – and a woman who did not have any children as they would be easier to subdue.

While she was out, he cut the phone lines and broke in through the back door. However, when she arrived home, she was accompanied by her brother William. Rader pretended to be an escaped felon and, threatening him with a .22, he ordered William to tie his sister up. He took William into another room and tied him up too.

Concerned that he might try and rescue his sister, he decided to strangle William first. When he fought back, Rader shot him. He intended to strangle or suffocate Kathryn when she was naked, or partially naked. But when she too struggled, he stabbed her.

William was not dead and, while Rader was slipping on Kathryn's blood, he made it out of the front door to call for help. Panicking, Rader fled. He tried to steal Kathryn's car, but it would not start. He could not get William's truck to start either, so he ran back to Wichita State University where he had left his car. Kathryn was still alive when the police arrived, but died from her wounds in hospital.

Inside job

On 12 November 1974, 23-year-old Sherry Baker was found dead less than three miles from the Otero house and just two miles from where

Kathryn Bright had lived. She was found face down on the living room floor, in her negligee and panties, with her hands bound behind her back with telephone cable torn from the wall; she had been gagged with a torn piece of a towel. As usual, the telephone line had been cut. The post-mortem revealed she had been stabbed over 60 times. A pair of scissors were found in the back of her neck. The blow had been so vicious that a blade broke.

Rader had installed the burglar alarm at her home, saying he 'rigged a home once that I felt like I could maybe get back in ... she hired our company to protect her home ... I think it's the only one I did.' He also admitted acts of petty theft while he was at work, saying: 'Nylons or socks, something they wouldn't miss. Have you ever been – I don't know, have you ever been in a woman's dresser? They got pantyhoses and hoses. They don't know what they got in there. You know, all you got to do is reach way back there and pick something out, they won't miss it.'

On 17 March 1977, Shirley Vian was the next victim. Rader was pursuing a woman named Cheryl who he had met in the Blackout Tavern near Wichita State University. This was Project Blackout. She was a single mother with a six-year-old son, but she was not at home. Then he saw a boy walking down the street. After he went into his home, Rader knocked on the door, posing as a detective. There were three children in the house. Rader switched off the TV and closed the blinds. Then their mother appeared from another room.

At gunpoint, he ordered the children to go into the bathroom and locked the door. He told Vian that he planned on having his way with her. To calm her down, he gave her a glass of water and smoked a cigarette with her. While the children were screaming in the bathroom, Rader tied her up, put a cord around her neck and strangled her. There was semen on her panties, which were found next to her body. In his confession, he said he would have killed the children too, if the phone had not rung.

Operation Fox Hunt was planned more carefully. Nancy Fox, he told investigators, appealed to him as a 'sexual female victim'. He recorded how he picked one target over another.

'The trolling stage was wide open. I might be looking and see someone else, say, well, this is even better yet ... and then I would drop this person, or I might leave them in the project box,' he wrote.

Dennis Rader.

'Usually once – once I got narrowed down and started homing in, it became a stalking stage ... but there's only been a couple that went the way I wanted them.'

He had studied her daily routine, what time she went to her two part-time jobs and her other habits. On 8 December 1977, he struck. As with Kathryn Bright and Sherry Baker, he cut the phone lines and broke in through the back door. He then rifled though her closet and drawers, stealing various items of clothing. When she returned home, he threatened her with a gun and told her that he was going to rape her and photograph her, but first he let her smoke a cigarette and go to the bathroom. Meanwhile, he began to undress.

She was still wearing a sweater, bra and panties when he handcuffed her and wrapped his belt around her legs, pulling it up and around her neck. Then he told her that he was BTK and he was going to kill her.

'And then she really, really squirmed and then ... and then I pulled, put the pressure down on it,' he said.

While being strangled, Nancy fought for her life and grabbed 'a hold of my nuts. Yeah, she did. And she was squeezing pretty hard. But it actually made me more excited.'

When she was dead, he took his belt, then tied her up with panty hose and scarves. He masturbated into her nightgown and threw it on the floor, next to her head. Then he left, taking with him some of her scarves, underwear and jewellery, which he later gave to his daughter when she was in high school. He stole her car to drive back to his own.

Evil poetry

On 10 February 1978, he wrote a four-page letter to the television station KAKE in Wichita describing the murders of the Oteros, Shirley Vian and Nancy Fox. In it, he enclosed a poem that parodied the lyrics of the American folk song 'Oh! Death'. It read:

OH! DEATH TO NANCY
What is this taht [sic] I can see,
Cold icy hands taking hold of me,
For Death has come, you all can see. Hell has open it,s [sic]
    gate to trick me.
Oh! Death, Oh! Death, can't you spare me, over for another
    year!
I'll stuff your jaws till you can't talk
I'll blind [sic] your leg's [sic] till you can't walk
  I'll tie your hands till you can't make a stand.
And finally I'll close your eyes so you can't see
I'll bring sexual death unto you for me.
B.T.K.

There had been another poem after the death of Shirley Vian which appears to have been in the partially suppressed letter in 1964. In the 1978 letter, he wrote: 'I find the newspaper not writing about the poem on Vian unamusing. A little paragraph would have enough. I know it not the media fault. The Police Chief he keep things quiet, and doesn't let the public know there a psycho running around lose strangling mostly women, there 7 in the ground; who will be next?'

He was plainly miffed that he was not getting the attention from the media that he thought he deserved. The letter continued:

'How many do I have to Kill before I get a name in the paper or some national attention. Do the cop think that all those deaths are not related? Golly-gee, yes the M.O. is different in each, but look a pattern is developing. The victims are tie up-most have been women-phone cut- bring some bondage mater sadist tendencies-no struggle, outside the death spot-no wintness except the Vain's Kids. They were very lucky; a phone call save them. I was go-ng to tape the boys and put plastics bag over there head like I did Joseph, and Shirley. And then hang the girl. God-oh God what a beautiful sexual relief that would been. Josephine, when I hung her really turn me on; her pleading for mercy then the rope took whole, she helpless; staring at me with wide terror fill eyes the rope getting tighter-tighter. You don't understand these things because your not under the influence of factor x). The same thing that made Son of Sam, Jack the Ripper, Havery Glatman, Boston Strangler, Dr. H.H. Holmes Panty Hose Strangler OF Florida, Hillside Strangler, Ted of the West Coast and many more infamous character kill. Which seem s senseless, but we cannot help it. There is no help, no cure, except death or being caught and put away. It a terrible nightmare but, you see I don't lose any sleep over it. After a thing like Fox I come home and go about life like anyone else. And I will be like that until the urge hit me again. It not continuous and I don't have a lot of time. It take time to set a kill, one mistake and it all over. Since I about blew it on the phone-handwriting is out-letter guide is to long and typewriter can be traced too. My short poem of death and maybe a drawing; later on real picture and maybe a tape of the sound will come your way. How will you know me. Before a murder or murders you will receive a copy of the initials B.T.K. , you keep that copy the original will show up some day on guess who?

'May you not be the unluck one! P.S. How about some name for me, its time: 7 down and many more to go. I like the following How about you?

'"THE B.T.K. STRANGLER", "WICHITA STRANGLER", "POETIC STRANGLER", "THE BOND AGE STRANGLER OR PSYCHO" "THE WICHITA HANGMAN THE WICHITA

EXECUTIONER", "THE GAROTE PHATHOM", "THE ASPHIXIATER". B.T.K'

At the time it was suggested that his poor spelling and lack of literacy was a ruse, disguising a highly intelligent man – which serial killers often are. But after he was arrested, the same standard of illiteracy appeared in his college work.

In 1979, he sent two identical packages, one to 63-year-old Anna Williams – intended victim in Project Pine Cone – who was not at home when he broke into her house, and the other to KAKE. These contained drawings of what he intended to do to his victim, some small items he had pilfered from Anna's home and another poem:

OH, ANNA WHY DIDN'T YOU APPEAR
Oh, Anna Why Didn't You Appear
T' was perfect plan of deviant pleasure so bold on that
    Spring nite
My inner felling hot with propension of the new awakening
    season
Warn, wet with inner fear and rapture, my pleasure of
    entanglement, like new vines at night
Oh, Anna, Why Didn't You Appear
Drop of fear fresh Spring rain would roll down from your
    nakedness to scent to lofty fever that burns within,
In that small world of longing, fear, rapture, and desparation,
    the game we play, fall on devil ears
Fantasy spring forth, mounts, to storm fury, then winter
    clam at the end.
Oh, Anna Why Didn't You Appear
Alone, now in another time span I lay with sweet enrapture
    garments across most private thought

Bed of Spring moist grass, clean before the sun, enslaved
with control, warm wind scenting the air, sun light
sparkle tears in eyes so deep and clear.
Alone again I trod in pass memory of mirrors, and ponder
why for number eight was not.
Oh, Anna Why Didn't You Appear
BTK

Apparently, Rader had broken into her home, as usual cutting the phone lines and forcing entry through the back door. He collected scarves, nylons, jewellery and panties from Anna's bedroom and that of her daughter. Scattering these alongside clothes on the floor he made a comfortable nest for himself, where he could wait for her. He lingered for several hours inside the home, not realizing that she had gone to her sister's for the evening. He eventually got tired of waiting and went away, leaving a note saying: 'Glad you weren't here, because I was.' Then he stole her car to drive back to where he had parked his own vehicle.

Missing from Boy Scout camp

Next time he would make no mistake. The victim, 53-year-old Marine Hedge, lived on the same street as Rader, just a few houses away, so he could keep an eye on her comings and goings. This appears to have taken years as she was killed eight years after the murder of Nancy Fox.

The local houses of women he was tracking looked to him like cookies, so Rader called the targeting, stalking and killing of Marine Hedge Operation Cookie. On the night of 26 April 1985, he cut the phone lines and broke into her house. When she returned home, she was with a male friend. He hid in the closet until 1am, when her friend had left and she had gone to sleep.

'She didn't wake up until I got into bed with her,' Rader said.

When she did, she found that he had already put his 'belt around her neck ... and throttled her to get her under control'. Once she was dead, he handcuffed her and took her underwear, stockings, her car keys and driver's licence, and some jewellery. Then he stripped her, wrapped her in blankets and put her in the trunk of her car. Then he drove to Christ Lutheran Church and put her in a basement room there that he had already prepared.

For several hours, he said he 'photographed her in bondage ... different poses for her'. Then he masturbated over her body. After he had cleaned up, he dumped her corpse, returned her car, retrieved his own and drove back to the Boy Scout camp he had been supervising earlier, slipping back in, so that no one noticed he had been missing.

Marine's son-in-law informed the police that she was missing. They found her car in a shopping centre. There was bed linen in the trunk that had otherwise been wiped clean. Her decomposing body was found in a ditch where people dumped trash. Rader said that he had returned to it several times to retrieve the ligatures he had used, but it was thought he actually returned to take more pictures of her naked corpse.

Rader had stalked 28-year-old Vicki Wegerle for three weeks. He supplemented his hit kit with a fake telephone-company ID, a hard hat and a tool belt. On 16 September 1986, he approached the elderly couple who lived next door to her, pretending to check their line. Then he moved on to Vicki's house and pretended to check her line, before pulling a gun from his briefcase.

Leaving her 18-month-old son to his own devices, he ordered her into the bedroom, where he tied her up. He said she was crying, but somehow broke the bonds he had been tying and fought back. She scratched his hands and arms while he strangled her. Once she was dead, he pulled her clothes off and masturbated, then posed her and took some photographs.

After that, he stole her car and dumped his briefcase and hard hat. Asked what he would have done if he'd been stopped by a police officer, he said: 'I hope I would have been faster than him with a gun.'

Vicki's body and distraught son were found by her husband when he came home for lunch.

Taunting words

In 1988, after the murders of three members of the Fager family in Wichita, a letter was received from someone claiming to be BTK. In it, he denied being the perpetrator in this case, but he credited the killer with doing admirable work. However, a week after Mrs Fager came home to find her husband and two daughters dead, Rader sent her a poem called 'Oh God He Put Kelli Sherri in the Tub'. Although the events related in the poem were accurate, the drawings of the bound and murdered girls were not. Mr Fager had been shot with a .357. Ten-year-old Sherri was found bound in the hot tub, where, it appears, she drowned. The naked body of her 16-year-old sister Kelli was put in the hot tub eight hours later. She had been strangled with a ligature and was dead when she was dumped in the water.

Next came the killing of 62-year-old Dolores Davis. This was called Project Dog-Side as she had a dog kennel on her property, which was just two blocks from Rader's home.

He had tried to break into her home several times. Once he had been repulsed by her cat, which caused such a commotion that it alerted Dolores. On the night of 19 January 1991, he used the cover of a Boy Scout winter camp to go about his lethal business. His parents were away, so he went to their house to change. Then he drove to the church where he had stashed his hit kit, and walked to Dolores's home.

He got in by throwing a cinder block through a sliding glass door, waking her. When she confronted him, he pretended to be an escaped convict on the run. What he wanted was some money and her car, so he could drive to California. He warned her that he had a gun and a knife, saying: 'Take your choice how you want it.'

He said he really wanted to spend some time with her, but once he had handcuffed her and tied her up, he strangled her with panty hose. When he was done with her, he put her body in the trunk of her car along with her driver's licence, a camera, a box of jewellery and some clothing. After he dumped her body, he returned the vehicle and walked back to the church to retrieve his car. Then he went to recover Dolores's body, which he stowed under a bridge, returning several times to take photographs of her tied up and wearing a mask to make her 'look prettier'. The mask, he explained, was the one he had used in self-bondage – 'I would try to take pictures, so I looked like maybe I was a female or a person in distress.'

There were other 'projects' that did not come off. Project Prairie was planned in a town in northeast Kansas when he was a census-taker. Again, he broke into a woman's house, but she was saved when she did not come home that evening. Rader wrote to the Wichita police about Project Bell on 8 December 2004. When Rader was finally arrested and his records seized, it was found that he detailed the habits and routines of hundreds of possible targets. Children were picked out as potential victims.

'If I could get a younger person or could have got a younger person I would do it,' he wrote. 'Just not sure, what's the term – like adults where they are attracted to kids: Paedophile, yeah. Probably have some of that in me ... occasionally I draw a kid tied up or something.'

Although there had been no murders he had claimed credit for since 1991, clearly Rader had been missing the attention. On 19 March 2004, the *Wichita Eagle* received an envelope containing the driver's licence of Vicki Wegerle and three photographs of her bound lying on the floor. The return address was 'Bill Thomas Killman ... 1684 South Oldmanor'. The name was fictitious and the address a vacant lot, but clearly it came from BTK.

In April, Wichita's KSN-TV received a letter allegedly from BTK, containing a photograph of an unidentified baby. Then on 4 May 2004, KAKE-TV received a fake ID card, a word puzzle and a list of chapters from 'The BTK Story' published by Court TV's Crime Library in 1999. Some of the chapter titles were changed, indicating that there might be more murders. The return address this time used the name Thomas B. King – or TBK.

Another list of chapters from 'The BTK Story', along with sheets from the chapter 'Death on a Cold January Morning' and pictures of naked women, bound, gagged and hanging were found taped to a stop sign in June. It also contained a graphic description of the Oteros' murder and a drawing entitled 'The Sexual Thrill Is My Bill', along with a proposed chapter list for his own version of 'The BTK Story' – 'Chapter One: A Serial Killer is Born'.

More bizarre material was found in the return slot of the Wichita Public Library, the UPS box and Nancy Fox's driver's licence was in another package found in Wichita's Murdock Park.

Another letter was in a cereal box dropped in a pick-up truck at Wichita's Home Depot, but the driver threw it out. However, it was retrieved from the garbage after Rader asked whether they had got it. A check of the CCTV at the parking lot showed the driver of a Jeep Cherokee dropping the box into the pick-up. Another cereal box was found in the countryside with a bound doll in it, while KAKE-TV got a series of postcards.

In a letter to the police, Rader asked whether, if he put further communications on computer disks, he could be traced. Naturally, in their reply in the *Wichita Eagle*, they said he could not, so, on 16 February 2005, he sent a floppy disk to KSAS-TV in Wichita, along with a copy of the cover of *Rules of Prey* by John Sandford, a novel about a serial killer.

On the disk there were traces of a deleted file. In the metadata, they found 'Christ Lutheran Church' and a record that it had last been modified by 'Dennis'. This led the police directly to Dennis Rader. But they needed more. Obtaining a medical sample from Rader's daughter, they found a partial match for the DNA left at the crime scenes. And when they went to arrest Rader on 25 February 2005, they found a Jeep Cherokee parked outside his house.

He waived his right to silence and spoke for over 30 hours before a court-appointed public defender shut him up. At the arraignment he kept silent, so not guilty pleas were entered on his behalf. But at the trial, he pleaded guilty to all ten charges of murder and was given ten life sentences without the possibility of parole.

In jail, he was kept in solitary confinement for his own protection. His wife was granted an emergency divorce, waiving the usual waiting period. However, his daughter Kerri stayed in touch and continued to write to him, though she found it difficult to reconcile the psychopathic killer with the loving father she knew.

'We were living our normal life,' she said. 'We looked like a normal American family because we were a normal family. And then everything upended on us.'

AILEEN WUORNOS: SPIDERWOMAN

ileen Wuornos never made any secret of the fact that she hated men. When she hung out in The Last Resort, a Hell's Angels bar in Port Orange, Florida, drinking and popping pills, she would curse all men and boasted that she would get even with this rotten masculine world.

The Hell's Angels put up with her and called her 'Spiderwoman' for the black leather outfits she wore. She was just another outcast like them. She had certainly come from a tough background.

Aileen Carol Wuornos was born in Rochester, Michigan on 19 February 1956, the second child of teenage parents Diane Wuornos and Leo Pitman. Her first recollections were of her mother screaming, while her alcoholic father dished out another brutal beating. When she was five, he abandoned his family. He was later sentenced to life imprisonment for raping a child and hanged himself in his prison cell. Her young mother, unable to stand her 'crying, unhappy babies', gave

Aileen and her elder brother Keith into the care of her parents, who adopted them.

Their grandparents were both alcoholics who spent little money on food. The children went hungry. Her grandfather would beat Aileen, forcing her to strip first. For fun 'Lee' – as she liked to call herself – and Keith used to like starting fires with lighter fuel. At the age of six, things went badly wrong and she suffered burns to her face, scarring her for life. She did poorly at school.

She began offering sexual favours to older boys in return for a sandwich and a drink. By the time she was 12, she was prostituting herself for beer and cigarettes, quickly moving on to drugs. A friend of the family raped her.

Aileen became pregnant before the age of 15 and her son was born in a Detroit maternity hospital on 23 March 1971 and was given up for adoption. When her grandmother died some months later, Aileen dropped out of school. Her grandfather killed himself and Keith turned to crime. By the age of 19, Aileen found herself all alone in the world and took to the road as a wandering prostitute, hitch-hiking from state to state.

In May 1974, at the age of 18, Aileen Wuornos – using the alias 'Sandra Kretsch' – was arrested in Colorado for disorderly conduct, drunk driving and firing a .22 pistol from a moving vehicle. She left town before her trial and returned to Michigan, where she was arrested for assault and disturbing the peace when she hurled a pool ball at a bartender. For this, and outstanding charges of driving without a licence and drinking while driving, she was fined $105.

At 20, she married a 69-year-old, beating him with his walking stick when he refused her constant demands for money. He took out a restraining order, then filed for divorce. When her brother Keith suddenly died from cancer, Aileen was surprised to receive an insurance payout of $10,000, but quickly squandered the money, buying a car which she promptly wrecked.

An end to loneliness

Back on the road, Aileen set off for Florida. She occasionally worked as a barmaid or cleaner, but her love of alcohol and drugs meant she could never hold down a job for long. She had no fixed abode and hitch-hiked around the highways of Florida, sleeping outdoors on the beach or at the roadside, supporting herself by prostitution, petty crime and forging cheques.

On 20 May 1981, she was arrested in Edgeworth for armed robbery of a convenience store, being released from prison in June 1983. Over the next two years, she faced numerous charges for passing forged cheques, car theft and driving offences. On many occasions, police found a firearm in her car.

The Last Resort was more of a home to her than anywhere else, despite its collection of souvenir panties and bras on the ceiling and walls papered with centrefolds. She sometimes slept on the porch or in the so-called Japanese hanging gardens, where the Angels hung despised Japanese motorcycles from the trees. She was known to one and all as a foul-mouthed, ill-tempered drunk.

In June 1986, Aileen met up with 22-year-old Tyria Moore in a gay bar in Daytona, Florida. It was a deeply romantic affair. Aileen believed Tyria would put an end to her loneliness, and that she would never abandon her as all the men in her life had. They were lovers for a year or so, but remained close companions for four years and were regularly in trouble as they drifted around Florida, living in trailer parks and seedy apartments. Most of the time, Aileen adopted the alias of 'Susan Blahovec'. She worked as a prostitute at truck stops and in bars, or thumbed lifts in pursuit of her trade. With clients, she was becoming increasingly belligerent and always carried a loaded pistol in her purse.

Trail of destruction

The two women had been spotted, though, and their descriptions were put into the Marion County computer. It matched the two women to six murders in the area. The victims were all men. Their bodies had been found dumped miles from where their cars had been found. Each had been shot with a small-calibre revolver and there was a condom wrapper left on the back seat of each of their cars.

The first had been in 1989 when a car belonging to 51-year-old electronics repairman Richard Mallory was found abandoned, his wallet and its contents scattered close by on 31 November. Two weeks later, his body, fully dressed, was found in woods northwest of Daytona Beach. He had been shot three times with a .22 pistol. On 1 June 1990, the naked corpse of 43-year-old David Spears was found in woodland 40 miles north of Tampa. He had been missing since 19 May and had been shot six times with a .22-calibre weapon.

Forty-year-old Charles Carskaddon vanished on 31 May somewhere on the road from Bonneville, Missouri. His naked body was found north of Tampa on 6 June. He had been shot nine times with a .22 pistol and his car was discovered the following day. His personal belongings, including his .45 automatic, had been stolen. Despite the similarities in these cases, the police still refused to recognize that a serial killer was at work in Florida.

Sixty-five-year-old Peter Siems was last seen when he left home near Palm Beach on 7 June, bound for Arkansas to visit relatives. On 4 July, his car was found, wrecked and abandoned, 200 miles to the north. Witnesses to the crash were able to describe two women leaving the vehicle, one blonde and one brunette. The blonde was bleeding from an injury, and a bloody palm print was obtained from the car trunk. As Siems was considerably older than the previous victims and an evangelical missionary, it was thought unlikely that he had accepted an offer of sex. It seemed that he had picked up two seemingly harmless hitch-hikers. According to leads, they were women matching descriptions from other crime scenes. One was stocky, the other thin with a tattoo on her arm.

Fifty-year-old Eugene Burress was reported missing from Ocala, in central Florida, on 30 July. His empty truck was found the following day. Then, nearly a week later, his badly decomposed body, fully clothed, was discovered by picnickers in Ocala National Forest. He had been shot twice with a .22 pistol. His credit cards had been scattered around and an empty cash bag from a local bank had been left at the scene.

Also missing from Ocala, on 11 September, was Dick Humphreys, a 56-year-old retired police chief from Alabama. The following day, his clothed body was discovered, shot seven times with a .22-calibre weapon. His car was found two weeks later, some 100 miles to the north, but was not traced to Humphreys until 13 October, when his badge and other personal items were discovered 70 miles to the southeast.

The corpse of 60-year-old Walter Antonio, a trucker and reserve police officer from Marritt Island, on Florida's east coast, was discovered near the northwest coast on 19 November. He was naked apart from his socks. His clothes were found later in a neighbouring county and his car back east on 24 November. He had been shot three times in the back and once in the head, and his police badge, baton, handcuffs and flashlight had all been stolen.

Intense media pressure at last forced the police to acknowledge that this was a series of related killings. It was thought that one or two women had been responsible for the deaths of the seven motorists largely along Interstate 75, which bisects Florida. The police published sketches of the two women seen fleeing the wreck of Peter Siems's car in the newspapers. Readers phoned in with the name of Tyria Moore and her lover Lee, along with various aliases she used.

Nowhere to hide

Over the next three weeks, searches of motel receipts uncovered the movements of 'Lee Blahovec', 'Lori Grody' and 'Cammie Greene', and fingerprint analysis identified the wanted woman as Aileen Wuornos. Meanwhile, she was raising money by pawning identifiable property stolen from her victims, leaving more tell-tale fingerprints.

Shortly after wrecking Peter Siems's car, Tyria had left Aileen and fled to Pennsylvania. In January 1991, the police traced her there and arrested her for auto theft. Valuable items belonging to the victims were found in her suitcase. Tyria broke down and blamed Aileen. She had lured her into a life of crime, Tyria said, and Aileen had murdered and robbed to buy her expensive gifts.

Aileen was picked up, asleep on the porch of The Last Resort. She thought she was being arrested on a five-year-old firearms charge. While Aileen was in jail, the police got Tyria to phone her, saying that she feared that the police were going to charge her with the murders.

'I'm not letting you go to jail,' Aileen said. She then confessed to the killings, saying that they were all done in self-defence as she feared being raped or killed. After her conviction, she admitted that this was a lie.

Usually, Aileen would be hitch-hiking when her victim stopped in his car to offer her a lift. Or sometimes she would pretend that her car had broken down and that, as a woman, she needed help. Either way, once in the car, she would offer to have sex with the man and get him to drive to a deserted spot. After sex, she would then take her vengeance on all mankind. She would kill the son-of-a-bitch, and rob him of his money and jewellery into the bargain. Even the hardened Hell's Angels were shocked that they had been harbouring a man-slayer.

Dragging Rose Bay near The Last Resort, the police found a .22, along with a torch and a handgun belonging to Walter Antonio.

Aileen Wuornos stood trial on 13 January 1992, charged with the murder of Richard Mallory. The star witness for the prosecution was Tyria Moore. As the only witness in her own defence, Wuornos took the stand and testified that she had been violently raped, sodomized, tortured and beaten by him, and that she had only shot him when he threatened to kill her. No evidence was presented regarding Mallory's character, and on 27 January, the jury found Aileen guilty. When they recommended the death penalty two days later, she cried out: 'I'm innocent! I was raped! I hope you get raped! Scumbags of America!'

Ten months later – and far too late – a TV reporter unearthed the fact that Mallory had indeed served ten years in another state for violent rape.

In April, Aileen pleaded guilty to the killing of Spears, Burress and Humphreys, and received the death penalty for all three. She also offered to reveal where the body of Peter Siems was hidden, but nothing was found and the police believed that this was merely a ruse to obtain a few days away from prison.

Aileen Wuornos, consistently proclaiming her innocence and lodging appeals, remained on death row in Florida for ten years, finally going to the electric chair on 9 October 2002.

MARY BELL: THE TYNESIDE STRANGLER

Known as 'The Tyneside Strangler', Mary Bell was just 11 years old when she was convicted of killing two young boys in 1968. It is hard to imagine that a child with anything approaching a normal, loving upbringing could have committed such heinous crimes at so young an age. Indeed, she was an unwanted and neglected child. When she was born on 26 May 1957, her 17-year-old mother Betty McCrickett rejected her, telling the midwife 'take the thing away from me'.

Mary's care was taken over by her grandmother. However, she could not escape the malign influence of her mother. Betty and later her husband Billy Bell, a violent alcoholic and habitual criminal, continued to live in the family home in Gateshead. At the age of just one, Mary nearly died under the wheels of a lorry in what would be the first of a series of puzzling accidents. To add to her distress, Betty and Billy threw Mary's grandmother out, so she was deprived of her emotional mainstay.

Betty said she could not cope with looking after her children and was often away. Mary was farmed out to relatives and friends, who noticed that she was cold and detached, and failed to bond with others.

When she was three, Betty took Mary to an adoption agency and gave her to a mentally unstable woman who had been prevented from adopting as she was emigrating to Australia. Betty's sister, who had followed her, got the child back, but Betty would not let her and her husband adopt the child. They noted that Mary never cried when she was hurt, but screamed and stamped when she did not get her own way. While she was not spanked at home, she resorted to violence from an early age. Once she threatened to bash her uncle's face in and hit him with a toy gun.

The family feared for Mary's life in her mother's care. Another uncle hurt his back, saving Mary when Betty dropped her from a first-floor window. On another occasion, Mary was rushed to hospital to have her stomach pumped, having taken an overdose of sleeping pills allegedly given to her by her mother. Five weeks later, a child who was out on the street with Mary was run over by a bus.

At kindergarten, Mary gained a reputation as an habitual liar; she was a disruptive influence and sometimes expressed a desire to hurt people. Told not to put her hands around another child's throat, she said: 'Why? Can I kill him?'

'The devil's spawn'

When Billy was arrested for armed robbery, Betty turned to prostitution as a dominatrix and used Mary as a prop in her sadomasochistic encounters. Soon, Mary said, she was forced into sexual acts with men. Despite her hating this, she was sharp enough to begin taking money on her own account, while her mother became increasingly violent, calling her daughter 'the devil's spawn'.

Clearly, with a background like that, things were not going to turn out well. There were sudden mood swings that made other children avoid her. However, she did find a soul mate – the daughter of a neighbour whose name was Norma Bell, though she was no relation. Norma was two years older, but Mary was the dominant one in the relationship.

On 11 May 1968, Mary and Norma were playing with a three-year-old boy on top of an air-raid shelter when the boy fell, cutting open his head. He said that one of the girls had pushed him, though he was not sure which. The next day, the mothers of three small girls, all about six, complained to the police that Mary had tried to choke them.

A constable visited. Both Mary and Norma denied pushing the boy off the air-raid shelter and trying to strangle the three girls. However, Norma said Mary had tried to throttle each of them, explaining: 'Mary went to one of the girls and said: "What happens if you choke someone; do they die?" Then Mary put both hands round the girl's throat and squeezed. The girl started to go purple. I told Mary to stop, but she wouldn't. Then she put her hands around Pauline's throat and she started going purple as well ... another girl, Susan Cornish, came up and Mary did the same thing to her.'

Mary was given a reprimand, though no charges were filed. Soon afterwards, Norma's father found Mary choking his daughter and had to give her a slap to make her release her grip.

Two weeks later, on the day before Mary's 11th birthday, two boys playing in an abandoned house found the body of four-year-old Martin Brown. When a local workman tried to administer CPR, Mary and Norma turned up and had to been ordered out when the police arrived. They then went to the home of Martin's aunt and told her: 'One of your sister's bairns has just had an accident. We think it's Martin, but we can't tell because there's blood all over him.'

As no cause of death was immediately apparent, it was assumed that the four-year-old had swallowed pills from a discarded bottle found nearby and the coroner's court returned an open verdict.

Later a local nursery school was broken into and vandalized. Investigating police found a note full of misspellings and obscenities. One jotting said: 'We did murder Martin Brown.' Another made the same admission and all of them mentioned murder. That same day, Mary drew a child in the same pose as Martin had been found in. She also noted that 'there had been a boy who just laid down and died'. Mary was the only pupil who made a reference to the dead boy.

A few days later, Mary turned up at the Brown residence. When his grieving mother told her he was dead, Mary said: 'Oh, I know. I wanted to see him in his coffin.'

The following day, there was another break-in at the nursery school. This time the police were alerted by a newly installed alarm. Nearby, they found Mary and Norma, who denied that they had been involved in the previous break-in. After they were released into the custody of their parents, Mary began spreading rumours that Norma had been responsible for the death of Martin Brown.

A second victim

On the afternoon of 31 July, three-year-old Brian Howe went missing. During the ensuing search, Mary told Brian's older sister that she had seen her brother playing near some concrete blocks on a vacant lot. His body was found there, barely covered in clumps of grass and weeds. He had been strangled and his legs, stomach and genitals had been mutilated with a pair of broken scissors found at the scene. This fact later convinced Detective Chief Inspector James Dobson that Mary was the killer.

A pathologist suggested that the killer was a child since little force had been used. All the children in the area were questioned. Mary said that she had seen Brian being beaten by an eight-year-old carrying a pair of broken scissors. She immediately came under suspicion as the discovery of the scissors had not been made public. Norma said that she had been with Mary when they stumbled across Brian's body and that Mary had admitted killing him.

At the police station, Norma confessed that she had been with Mary when she attacked the boy but had run away when she had 'gone all funny' and began strangling him. She had returned to find Mary cutting his hair and legs, and mutilating his penis with the scissors. A razor blade had also been used to carve the letter 'N', later amended to 'M', on the child's stomach. Norma told the police that the razor blade could be found under a rock, where they recovered it.

Confronted with this, Mary demanded to see a solicitor and accused the police of brainwashing her. She then retaliated by accusing Norma of the murder of Brian Howe.

In the statement she gave to the police, Mary said: 'Brian started to cry and Norma asked him if he had a sore throat. She started to squeeze his throat and he started to cry. She said: "This isn't where the lady comes, it's over there, by them big blocks." We went over to the blocks and she says: "Ar – you'll have to lie down," and he lay down beside the blocks where he was found. Norma says: "Put your neck up," and he did. Then she got hold of his neck and said: "Put it down." She started to feel up and down his neck. She squeezed it hard; you could tell it was hard because her fingertips were going white. Brian was struggling, and I was pulling her shoulders, but she went mad. I was pulling her chin up, but she screamed at me.

'By this time, she had banged Brian's head on some wood or corner of wood and Brian was lying senseless. His face was all white and bluey, and his eyes were open. His lips were purplish and had all like slaver on, it turned into something like fluff. Norma covered him up and I said: "Norma, I've got nothing to do with this, I should tell on you, but I'll not ..."

'Norma was acting kind of funny and making twitchy faces and spreading her fingers out. She said: "This is the first, but it'll not be the last." I was frightened then ... Norma went into the house and she got a pair of scissors and she put them down her pants. She says: "Go and get a pen." I said: "No, what for?" She says: "To write a note on his stomach," and I wouldn't get the pen. She had a Gillette razor blade. It had Gillette on. We went back to the blocks and Norma cut his hair. She tried to cut his leg and his ear with the blade.'

Forensics found grey fibres from Mary's woollen dress on the bodies of both Brian and Martin's bodies, and maroon fibres from Norma's skirt were found on Brian's shoes. When Brian's coffin was brought out for the funeral procession, Mary was standing there. DCI Dobson said: 'She stood there, laughing. Laughing and rubbing her hands. I thought: "My God, I've got to bring her in. She'll do another one."'

Both Mary and Norma were charged with murder. They were tried at Newcastle Assizes in December 1968. Both pleaded not guilty and testified in their own defence. Despite their young age, the judge allowed the press to print their names and photographs.

Norma admitted that she had not alerted some boys who were nearby when Mary had started strangling Brian.

'I did not know what was going to happen in the first place,' she said, insisting she had 'never touched' the child. Clearly, she was believed and was acquitted of all charges.

In his summing-up, the judge, Mr Justice Cusack, said of Mary: 'She has told four stories and, having told four stories, it is inconceivable that the jury would believe any one of them. She had fabricated. She is a very sick child. One can only hope that she can be given treatment to help her.'

However, the jury found Mary Bell guilty only of manslaughter on the grounds of diminished responsibility. She was detained at Her Majesty's pleasure as it was judged that she was a grave risk to other children. Released in 1980, she was given a new identity and has gone on to become a mother and a grandmother.

Eighteen years after her release, Mary Bell co-operated with distinguished journalist, Gitta Sereny, who had already published *The Case of Mary Bell* in 1972, to write *Cries Unheard: the Story of Mary Bell*. In it, she revealed the grizzly story of her early childhood, but that did not assuage her guilt, as she herself pointed out: 'There are many unhappy, very disturbed kids out there who don't end up robbing families of their children.'

KEITH HUNTER JESPERSON: THE HAPPY FACE KILLER

Known as 'The Happy Face Killer', Keith Hunter Jesperson adorned his numerous anonymous confessions with happy faces – a circle with two dots for eyes and a broad crescent smile – in the days before emojis became de rigueur.

Born in Chilliwack, British Columbia in 1955, Jesperson suffered at the hands of a violent and abusive father, and was shunned by his brothers and sisters. His father charged him $30 a week for bed and board, while his siblings lived for free. His brothers nicknamed him 'Igor' or 'Ig', which made him an outcast at high school. Soon he was setting fire to things.

Like many serial killers, he began his murderous career as a child, torturing and killing small animals. Then he graduated to killing stray dogs and cats in the trailer park where they lived to gain the approval of his dad. Soon, he was fantasizing about killing people.

At the age of ten, he had a friend called Martin. They would often get into trouble together and Martin would frequently blame Keith for things he had done. This led Keith to attack Martin, violently beating him until his father pulled him away. He later claimed to have meant to kill the boy. A year later, Jesperson was swimming in a lake when another boy held him underwater until he blacked out. Some time later at a public pool, Jesperson took his revenge, attempting to drown the boy by holding his head underwater until the lifeguard stepped in.

He had another ambition – to become a Royal Canadian Mounted Policeman – but he was thwarted by an injury he sustained during training. After moving to the United States, he became a long-haul truck driver. At 20, he married. The couple had three children but divorced in 1990.

During his marriage, his cruelty to animals did not stop. His daughter Melissa said he killed stray cats and gophers that wandered near their farmhouse. One day when she was five, she watched, horrified, as he hanged kittens she had found in the cellar from the family's clothes line and beat them. He laughed as the kittens clawed each other trying to make their escape, and enjoyed her screams and pleas. She ran to get her mother and, when they returned, the kittens lay dead on the ground.

There was no surprise then when, while he was out on the road, his wife packed up her things and her children's belongings and went to live with her parents 200 miles away in Spokane, Washington.

Made-up story

The marriage had irretrievably broken down when, on 22 January 1990, he met 23-year-old Taunja Bennett in a bar in Portland, Oregon. They went back to a house he was renting and had sex. Afterwards they argued and he strangled her with a rope. He went back to the bar to establish an alibi, before dumping her half-naked body on a country road.

Fifty-seven-year-old Laverne Pavlinac read about the case and cooked up a way to rid herself of her abusive live-in boyfriend John

Sosnovske. She told the police that he had killed Taunja Bennett. When the police proved sceptical, she told them that he had forced her to watch while he raped and murdered Bennett, and helped him dispose of the body. He was charged with murder, she with abetting him. Fearing the death penalty, he pleaded 'no contest' and was sentenced to life, eligible for parole after 15 years. She got ten years. This was rather longer than she had anticipated and she began to claim that she had made up the story. No one would listen.

Meanwhile, Jesperson would later blame his father's bragging about the stray cats and dogs he killed for the murder.

'All this did is spawn in me the urge to kill again,' he said. 'I began to think of what it would be like to kill a human being. The thought stayed with me for years, until one night it happened. I killed a woman by beating her almost to death and finished her off by strangulation. No longer did I search for animals to mistreat. I now looked for people to kill. And I did. I killed over and over until I was caught.'

Perhaps miffed that he was not getting the attention he deserved for the murder of Taunja Bennett, Jesperson wrote on a wall in the men's room of a Greyhound bus depot in Livingston, Montana: 'I killed Taunja Bennett January 21, 1990, in Portland, Oregon. I beat her to death, raped her and loved it. I'm sick but I enjoy myself too. Two people took the blame and I'm free.'

Alongside this was a 'happy face'.

A few days later, in the men's room at a truck stop in Umatilla, Oregon, he wrote: 'I killed Taunja Bennett in Portland. Two people got the blame so I can kill again.' Once more, there was a happy face.

However, these messages gave the police few clues to go on. Besides, two people had already been found guilty and were in prison.

True to his word, Jesperson did go on to kill again. On 30 August 1992, the body of an unidentified woman was found ten miles outside Blythe, California. She had been raped and strangled. Jesperson called her Claudia, saying: 'There was Claudia, a girl wanting a ride to

95

Phoenix, Arizona with me. She tried to extort my wallet from me and died trying.'

A month later, the body of Cynthia Lyn Rose was found in Turlock, California. Jesperson claimed that she was a prostitute working the truck stop there who had climbed into his truck while he was sleeping.

Attention-seeker

Around this time, he began writing to Phil Stanford, a columnist for *The Oregonian*, claiming that he had killed Cynthia Rose and other women. His letters were signed off with a 'happy face'. Stanford quickly dubbed the author 'The Happy Face Killer'.

His fourth victim was another prostitute, 26-year-old Laurie Ann Pentland of Salem, Oregon. Her body was found in November 1992 behind a store in Salem. She had been strangled. According to Jesperson, she tried to double the fee they'd agreed for sex. When she threatened to call the police, he killed her. DNA and other forensic evidence would link him to the corpse. He claimed that she made contact with him via citizen's band radio and they had sex several times.

'I felt so much power,' he wrote as The Happy Face Killer. 'I then told her she was going to die and slowly strangled her.'

The following July, another woman's body was found west of Santa Nella, California on a state highway near a route used by truckers. She had been dead for a couple of days and the county coroner initially listed her death as a drug overdose. The case was reopened after The Happy Face Killer wrote another letter confessing. It referred to her as a 'street person'.

On 14 September 1994, another unidentified body was found by a road crew alongside Interstate 10 outside Crestview, Florida. The remains consisted largely of bones. The best the coroner could do was determine that she was about 40 when she had died. Jesperson called her 'Susanne'.

In January 1995, he picked up 21-year-old Angela Subrize in Spokane, Washington and agreed to give her a lift to Fort Collins, Colorado. On the way, she changed her mind and asked him to take her to Indiana instead. Jesperson said that he became enraged because Angela would not have sex with him when they had stopped at a truck stop just east of Cheyenne, Wyoming. She kept 'bitching' at him to keep driving in bad weather, so he strangled her by pressing his fist against her throat. Then he went to sleep in peace.

When he awoke three hours later, he drove on into Nebraska and pulled off into a rest area where he bound her body with black nylon rope and tied it face down under his rig. He dragged it along the road for about ten to twelve miles 'to grind off her face and prints'. Then he untied her body and threw it into a ditch along Interstate 80, near Gothenberg, some 250 miles east of Cheyenne. The nylon rope was still attached to her ankles when her body was found in September. It was so badly decayed she was only identified by pelvic X-rays and a tattoo of Tweety Bird – aka Tweety Pie – making an obscene gesture on one of her ankles.

Despite Happy Face boasting about his murders in the press, the police were none the wiser until Jesperson murdered his long-time girlfriend, 41-year-old Julie Ann Winningham, who, he came to think, was only staying with him for his money. He strangled her on 10 March 1995, dumping her nude body on an embankment alongside State Highway 14 just east of the Clark and Skamania County line in Washington. Naturally, he was a person of interest in the case.

The police close in

Checking with the trucking company he was working for, the police discovered that he was on the road to Pennsylvania. Then he was heading on to Texas, New Mexico and Arizona. On 22 March, Detective Rick Buckner of Clark County Sheriff's Department flew

Keith Jesperson.

to Las Cruces, New Mexico, where he spent six hours questioning Jesperson, who refused to talk. With nothing to go on, the police had to release him.

Nevertheless, Jesperson was convinced that he was going to be arrested. Twice he tried to kill himself by attempting to overdose on sleeping pills. Both times he awoke.

Writing to his brother, he said: 'Seems like my luck has run out. I will never be able to enjoy life on the outside again. I got into a bad situation and got caught up with emotion. I killed a woman in my truck during an argument. With all the evidence against me, it looks like I truly am a black sheep. The court will appoint me a lawyer and there will be a trial. I am sure they will kill me for this.

'I am sorry that I turned out this way. I have been a killer for five years and have killed eight people, assaulted more. I guess I haven't learned anything.

'Dad always has worried about me because of what I have gone through in the divorce, finances, etc. I have been taking it out on different people ... As I saw it, I was hoping they would catch me. I took 48 sleeping pills last night, and I woke up well rested. The night before, I took two bottles of pills to no avail. They will arrest me today.'

After putting the letter in the mail, he called Detective Buckner from Cochise County, Arizona and confessed to the murder of Julie Winningham. Six days later, Buckner flew to Arizona to arrest him and bring him back to Washington. Arriving there, he called his brother and begged him to destroy the letter. However, on legal advice, his brother decided to turn the letter over to the police as it would be unlawful to destroy or to hold on to evidence. The handwriting matched that in the letters Stanford had received.

Shortly after the letter was turned over to the police, it was published by a number of newspapers. It was the beginning of a major flirtation with the media.

'I was Arnold Schwarzenegger,' Jesperson bragged to a reporter about his childhood experiences. 'It was like I was playing war. When I looked at those dogs, they would squat and pee. They'd be so scared that they'd tremble.'

By his own admission, Jesperson enjoyed the fear he instilled in these animals, and took great pleasure in watching and feeling the life literally drain out of them as they succumbed to death. It was an obsession.

'You come to the point where killing something is nothing. It's the same feeling,' he said, whether he was strangling a human being or an animal. 'You've already felt the pressure on the throat of them trying to grab air. You're actually squeezing the life out of these animals and there isn't much difference. They're gonna fight for their lives just as much as a human being will.'

Buckner contacted law enforcement agencies around the country and asked them to open their cold-case files on female homicide victims found near major highways and truck stops. He needn't have bothered. Jesperson told his attorney about his murders. Although he was advised to keep quiet, Jesperson refused to keep his own counsel. He wanted to be prevented from killing more women.

Later, he gave more details to the press, signing his letters with his trademark happy face. He admitted to 160 murders, but recanted on many of his confessions, some of which were clearly fanciful. Only eight have been confirmed. He pleaded guilty to the murder of Julie Ann Winningham, Taunja Bennett, Laurie Ann Pentland and Angela Subrize, earning himself four life sentences. This meant Laverne Pavlinac and John Sosnovske were released after serving four years.

From prison, Jesperson would joke about murder, even offering a 'Self-Start Serial Killer Kit'.

'This is the offer you all have been dying for! The Self-Start Serial Killer Kit,' he wrote. 'Now you can be the only serial killer on your block ... learn from a professional serial killer! Get rid of that unwanted family member! Get that job you always wanted by opening up the slot ... Everyone will be dying to meet you ... You get a full life Julie Winningham Look-alike Doll with an extra tough spring-back neck, so you will soon have the strength to squeeze the shit out of anyone.'

BRUCE MCARTHUR: THE TORONTO SERIAL KILLER

A grandfather in his 60s, Bruce McArthur escaped detection because he did not fit the profile of a serial killer. Michael Arntfield, a criminologist at the University of Western Ontario, who studies all solved and unsolved murders in North America going back 50 years, pointed out that murders committed by people aged 60 or older account for fewer than two per cent of the total. None of them include serial sexual offenders like McArthur.

Arrested in 2018, aged 67, McArthur pleaded guilty to eight murders. The first was in 2010 when he was 58. This has led criminologists such at Arntfield to assume that he must have begun his murderous career some time earlier. But no previous homicide has been ascribed to him despite the largest investigation ever conducted by the Toronto Police Service, which also called on the resources of the Ontario Provincial Police, Royal Canadian Mounted Police and other police and forensic services.

Born in 1951 in rural Ontario, McArthur felt that he had suffered at the hands of his strict Scottish Presbyterian father because he sensed his son's incipient homosexuality. Perhaps as a riposte, McArthur married his childhood sweetheart in 1974 at the age of 23. They had two children. They moved to a suburb of Toronto where he was a pillar of the church and worked as a buyer for Eaton's department store, just a few blocks from the city's burgeoning gay village. Homosexuality had been decriminalized in Canada in 1969.

Between 1975 and 1978, 14 men from Toronto's gay community turned up dead. Half of the cases were solved; the others went cold. Detective Sergeant Hank Idsinga, lead investigator on the McArthur case, said: 'Would it surprise me if Mr McArthur was linked to some murders from his late twenties? It wouldn't.' But no positive link has ever been established.

He quit Eaton's in 1978 to become a travelling salesman, selling socks and underwear. This may have presented opportunities.

'I'm being completely hypothetical here,' said clinical psychologist Dr John Bradford, who examined the case after McArthur was arrested. 'But let's make an assumption: This is a guy that's travelled around a bit. He's been a salesman, which puts him in a situation where he could find vulnerable victims. But let's assume for argument's sake that he may have started in his late-30s and there may have been one incident every five years and he's now looking at 20 or 30 years [of potential homicides].'

And he could easily have got away with it.

'If you dump a body in Northern Ontario, it's pretty much lights out,' Arntfield said. 'There's a good chance they're never going to find the remains.'

Major life change

At the age of 40, McArthur began cheating on his wife with men and came out a year and a half later. He and his wife continued living together, eventually separating after 25 years of marriage. At that time, he began seeing a psychiatrist and was on Prozac for about six months.

He then had a four-year relationship with a man. They lived together, but broke up when his boyfriend refused to commit. Around the same time, McArthur went bankrupt and finally got a divorce.

McArthur was just turning 50 in 2001 when he answered a small ad in a gay magazine. It had been placed by actor and model Mark Henderson, who let McArthur into his apartment around noon on 31 October to show him his Halloween costume. McArthur struck him from behind several times with the metal pipe that he said he carried to protect himself from street hustlers. Henderson fought back before losing consciousness. When he came round, he called 911 and was taken to St Michael's Hospital. There, it was found that he had suffered injuries to his head and body. He needed several stitches to the back of his head and his fingers as well as six weeks of physiotherapy.

After handing himself in, McArthur pleaded guilty to charges of assault with a weapon and assault causing bodily harm. He apologized to the victim and said he did not remember the attack and wondered whether he was suffering an epileptic seizure at the time. He was given a conditional sentence of two years less a day, which would see McArthur spend the first year under house arrest, followed by a curfew for six months. The sentence would be followed by three years' probation. During the sentence, McArthur was barred from the downtown area that included Toronto's gay village to prevent him from endangering male sex workers. He was also barred from owning a gun for ten years and his DNA was added to the police database.

A psychiatric report prepared for the case concluded that his 'risk for violence is very minimal'. This proved not to be the case. Indeed, he signed up to gay dating sites, asking for 'submissive men of all ages'. He told potential sexual partners that he was looking to 'see how much you can take' and promising to 'push till you can't take anymore'.

A regular on the gay scene, his Facebook page showed him partying, particularly with young men of South Asian or Middle Eastern heritage. Working as a self-employed landscape gardener, he frequently employed young men of a similar background. They also appeared in nude photographs in his bathroom according to a friend of his son Todd, who came to stay with him after being jailed for 14 months for making obscene phone calls. The men had erections and the friend said Todd had told him they were acquaintances of his father. By then, McArthur had moved into a neighbourhood largely populated by immigrants.

Anonymous tip-off

In November 2012, Project Houston was set up under Detective Sergeant Idsinga to investigate the disappearance of Skanda Navaratnam, Abdulbasir Faizi and Majeed Kayhan from Toronto's gay village. After an anonymous tip-off, McArthur was interviewed as a potential witness. He admitted knowing Navaratnam and Faizi, also saying that he had employed Kayhan in his landscaping business and had a sexual relationship with him, which he broke off.

It transpired that Navaratnam, a 40-year-old Tamil refugee, had also worked for McArthur and had had a sexual relationship with him. They had met ten years before he disappeared, leaving his newly acquired dog behind the bar in a gay bar called Zippers. The police had briefly investigated a possible link between Navaratnam's murder and convicted killer Luka Magnotta (see page 111).

Forty-two-year-old Faizi was an Afghan immigrant. His car was found abandoned near a popular cruising spot for gay men and, coincidentally, near McArthur's apartment. Fifty-eight-year-old Kayhan was also an immigrant from Afghanistan, who had fled with his wife and children during the Soviet–Afghan War. The couple had since divorced. Neither man had come out to his family.

Nothing connected McArthur to the missing men and, in 2014, after he had already committed three murders, McArthur was granted a record suspension, which meant his criminal past would no longer be shown on background checks.

On 26 June 2017, 49-year-old Andrew Kinsman disappeared after attending Pride Toronto, leaving his cat in his apartment without food and water. He had known McArthur for at least ten years after being the barman at the Black Eagle, a gay bar where McArthur hung out.

Earlier that year, 44-year-old Turkish immigrant Selim Esen had gone missing. He had no fixed abode, sofa-surfing with friends after being kicked out by his boyfriend. Esen had recently completed a week-long course on peer counselling at St Stephen's community house. McArthur was also a client there. A new investigation, Project Prism, was set up to investigate the disappearance of Kinsman and Esen, and to look into whether there were any links to the unsolved disappearances five years earlier investigated by Project Houston. Project Prism was again headed by Detective Sergeant Idsinga.

His caseload expanded on 29 November when the body of 22-year-old Tess Richey was found in a stairwell after a night out in Toronto's gay village four days earlier. The next day, the body of Alloura Wells, a homeless transgender woman, was identified, although her body had been found in August. However, Toronto's chief of police, Mark Saunders, assured the public that there was no evidence that a serial killer was at work.

In the Kinsman case, at last the police had something to go on. The name 'Bruce' was written against 26 June on a calendar in Kinsman's apartment. Checking the CCTV footage from the camera outside Kinsman's block, the police identified someone matching his appearance getting into a red 2004 Dodge Caravan. Although neither the face of the driver nor the licence plate were clearly visible, a vehicle of that make and description had been registered to Bruce McArthur. He had since sold it for scrap, but, fortunately, the police tracked it down before it was crushed and they found traces of blood. It turned out to be Kinsman's. Esen's DNA was also found.

Secrets of the apartment

The investigation went into overdrive. After obtaining a warrant, the

Police investigating a property where Bruce McArthur worked.

police surreptitiously entered McArthur's apartment and cloned his computer's hard drive. Among the deleted files they found pictures of the missing men – dead. They were posed, naked except for a hat or fur coat, sometimes with their eyes taped open and a cigar dangling from their lips. Some of their heads or beards had been shaved and McArthur kept the hair as a trophy, along with jewellery and a notebook.

McArthur was put under 24-hour surveillance, with instructions that he should be arrested immediately if he was seen alone with anyone. On 18 January 2018, a young man was seen entering his apartment. Fearing for his safety, the police entered the flat to find him handcuffed to the bed. McArthur was trying to tape his mouth shut and put a plastic bag over his head. The victim was an immigrant from the Middle East. Again, he was married and had not told his family he was gay. They had met through a dating app and they had had sex several times before.

McArthur was arrested and charged with the murders of Kinsman and Esen. The problem was, their bodies had not been found. The search was on. Forensic teams scoured properties where McArthur had been landscaping. They found the dismembered bodies of three men in large planter pots. Charges were laid against McArthur for the murder of Majeed Kayhan, Soroush Mahmudi, who had disappeared in 2015, and Dean Lisowick, a homeless man who had never been reported missing.

Fifty-year-old Mahmudi was a refugee from Iran. He had been reported missing by his wife, but his family knew of no connection between him and the Toronto gay scene. However, before his marriage, he had had a four-year relationship with a transgendered woman. Lisowick was 44 and a resident of Toronto's shelter system. An addict, he had supported his habit by working as a male prostitute.

Soon afterwards, the police found three more bodies in planters, including that of Andrew Kinsman, but the cadaver dogs were having trouble in unearthing any more because the ground was frozen. Kinsman's body was identified by fingerprints, while those of Navaratnam and Mahmudi were identified from dental records. Charges followed.

A seventh set of remains was discovered in a planter and the police released the picture of another alleged victim in the hope that someone would recognize him. McArthur was charged with an eighth count of first-degree murder to do with the death of Kirushna Kumar Kanagaratnam. Another Tamil refugee from Sri Lanka, he had disappeared in 2015, but no one had reported him missing because he was on the run from a deportation order.

McArthur pleaded guilty to eight charges of first-degree murder. Noting his lack of remorse, the judge sentenced him to life imprisonment with no eligibility for parole for 25 years when he would be 91. As he was overweight and suffered from Type 2 diabetes, it was unlikely he would live that long.

The police came in for criticism over their investigation as McArthur had been on the loose for eight years since his first known murder. They had also missed a trick in 2016 when McArthur and an unidentified man who he met through a dating app were masturbating each other in the back of McArthur's van in a McDonald's restaurant parking lot. McArthur allegedly began throttling the man who broke free, saying he was going to the police. It seems that McArthur followed him to a police station, or went there while the man phoned police. McArthur told the police the man had choked him, or that the incident was consensual. The man had asked to be choked, then panicked and fled. However, McArthur was not charged and was released after his story was deemed credible. No report was filed. Homicide investigators only became aware of the alleged incident after McArthur's arrest when the man came forward again to report it. McArthur had pictures of this man. In some, he was wearing a fur coat similar to the one in which McArthur posed his victims.

Similarly, his conviction for the attack on Mark Henderson had not come up on background checks. The police were accused of being lackadaisical in their investigation because the victims were gay and not white.

'This is something that hasn't happened in our city before. We've sat back and watched CNN and watched news reports on serial killers in other countries, but we haven't seen it here,' said Police Chief Saunders. 'We knew that people were missing and we knew we didn't have the right answers. But nobody was coming to us with anything. If things are not reported, it emboldens the suspect.'

LUKA MAGNOTTA: KITTEN KILLER

Luka Magnotta was not a serial killer. He only had one human victim. However, he seems to have had the makings of one and, if he had not been caught thanks to the amateur detective work of internet sleuths, he might have gone on to become one.

His story began on 25 October 2010 when a video called *1 boy 2 kittens* was posted on YouTube. It showed an unidentified man deliberately suffocating two kittens, using a sealed plastic bag and a vacuum cleaner. Then a video showing a kitten being eaten by a python was posted, followed by a video of a kitten duct-taped to a broom handle being drowned in a bath. Animal rights organizations were outraged and offered a reward for information leading to the perpetrator's arrest. Later, they posted a YouTube video claiming that he was the 'Hollywood Sign Murderer' in an attempt to flush him out.

In January 2012, the head of 66-year-old Hervey Medellin had been found in a plastic bag near the Hollywood sign on the hills overlooking

Los Angeles. Later, a right hand and a foot were found in a shallow grave nearby. After a search of the area, a left hand was also found. The day before Medellin's head was discovered, his boyfriend Gabriel Campos-Martinez filed a missing persons report after the police visited the apartment the two men shared following an anonymous tip that Medellin was missing. Campos-Martinez initially said that Medellin had gone to Mexico. It transpired that, when Medellin had wanted to break off the relationship, Campos-Martinez had killed him. Medellin had died of asphyxiation on or about 27 December 2011. Shortly before the murder, a computer in the apartment the men shared had been used to access an article on dismembering human bodies: 'Butchering of the Human Carcass for Human Consumption'. Campos-Martinez was sentenced to 25 years to life.

Internet investigators formed a Facebook group to look into the case of the YouTube cat killer. Deanna Thompson, a data analyst at a large casino in Las Vegas, took an interest. She noted that the one person in the group who was sticking meticulously to investigating the facts was a man named John Green. He took a forensic interest in the room where the kitten killing took place. It was small and cramped, approximately eight feet by ten. You could see a door, a bed and a table. Green realized that things like door handles and electric sockets were different in different countries, so there might be enough clues in the videos to track down the perpetrator.

The bedspread had a wolf's head on it. He discovered that it was made by a company in North America. One had sold on eBay, but he couldn't see who the buyer was. It was shipped internationally, so that was no help.

There were some voices in the background, so it seemed there was more than one person in the room. A Ukrainian member of the group realized that they were speaking Russian. Thompson then noticed that the talking suddenly stopped, like one of the people had left the room.

Then she realized that there was a click – the voices were a recording of a Russian sitcom. She had spent 16 hours looking at various doorknobs from Lithuania to no avail. A couple of pictures posted with the video showed the perpetrator playing with the kittens, but his face was pixilated. The kitten-killer was fooling with them.

Searching through the video frame by frame, Thompson spotted a pack of cigarettes. It had on it a warning from the US Surgeon General, so the action probably took place in North America. She also saw the yellow vacuum cleaner used to suck the air out of the vacuum-sealed bag, killing the two kittens. She posted the picture to a vacuum-cleaner forum that immediately identified it as a model only sold in North America.

Fitting the profile

A psychologist studying criminal profiling recognized that the perpetrator was getting excitement out of acts of cruelty on helpless animals. The group realized that, when the excitement of cat-killing wore off, the killer would go after other prey. Serial killers, including Ian Brady, Jeffrey Dahmer, Jim Jones and Keith Jesperson, began

An image from Magnotta's YouTube video.

by torturing and killing cats. The kitten killer was on their way to becoming a serial killer and had to be stopped. But the warning members of the Facebook group sent to the police went unheeded. They were dismissed as internet nerds.

It was also clear that the kitten killer craved attention. Then it was found that a 'Jamet Cramsalot Inhisass' had posted a video of a kitten being burned alive in a cage on his Facebook page. One of the investigators got the idea of simply asking whether he was the guy who had done the other kitten killings. He replied: 'Yes, I kill kittens LOL. And there's nothing you can do about it.'

They thought they had found the right person, but then found out that this was just an internet troll, a would-be copycat with mental problems. Then, out of nowhere, came the message that the person they were looking for was named Luka Magnotta. There were hundreds of pictures of him on the internet from around the world with unbelievable stories attached. The guy was a long-lost cousin of River Phoenix. He was dating Madonna.

They found an audition tape for a reality TV show about male models featuring Luka Magnotta made three years earlier. It identified him as a Canadian. Green noticed that, in the photos, the skin tone of the face did not match that of the body. Sometimes they did not line up properly. One post was about him getting married to a girl in Russia. A member of the group managed to find the original wedding photograph. He had been using Photoshop to add his face to it and other pictures.

Man of many guises

Eric Newman, alias Luka Rocco Magnotta, was a model, stripper and escort who appeared in gay porn videos. He had created many profiles on various internet social media sites and discussion forums over several years, and had come to public attention by denying that he was dating notorious murderer Karla Homolka. The wife of convicted serial killer Paul Bernardo, she was infamous in Canada. They were known as the Ken and Barbie killers after raping and murdering three 14-year-old girls, one of whom was her sister. In a controversial plea bargain, Karla was convicted only of manslaughter and sentenced to just 12 years in exchange for testifying against her husband.

A rumour that he was dating her had been planted by Magnotta himself, it was discovered later. Joe Warmington, a journalist with the *Toronto Sun*, got in touch with him. They met and Warmington said Magnotta bore a striking resemblance to Bernardo.

'My modelling career has gone downhill these days, to be honest with you,' complained Magnotta. 'And it's all because of this whole rumour of me dating Karla Homolka. The rumour's destroyed my life, basically, and ... I want to set the record straight that me and her have absolutely no connection.'

Not only was the rumour costing him work, it was also a threat to his life, he said. His address had been posted online and he had had to move. He claimed he was about to have a nervous breakdown. The problem was that the interview with Warmington was three years before the first cat-killing video, so they were no closer to finding out where he was.

They then looked through all the pictures he had posted, looking for Exif data – metadata tags provided by digital cameras and smartphones that recorded the date, time and GPS when the photograph was taken. One of the pictures showed Magnotta sitting on a chaise longue in a department store. The Exif data said the photograph was taken in the Toronto Eaton Shopping Centre on 25 October 2010 – the day the first kitten-killing video was posted.

Green was determined to discover Magnotta's address. In one picture on the internet, he was shown on a balcony on the third or fourth floor. Behind him is an intersection with a Petro-Canada gas station on the corner. In a blog post, he complained about the paparazzi harassing him outside his condominium in Etobicoke, a suburb outside Toronto. There were six Petro-Canada gas stations there. Using Street View on Google Earth, Green quickly identified which one it was. Across the road from it was an apartment block – 304 Mill Street. The police took some persuading, but eventually they went there. A Luka Magnotta had lived there, but the police were told that he had since moved to Russia. With the investigation stalled, the Facebook group dwindled from 15,000 to 8,000.

Meanwhile Alex West, a journalist for the *Sun* newspaper, tracked Magnotta to the Fusilier Inn, a cheap hotel in north London. He complained that he was getting death threats after being accused of killing kittens – a thing he denied doing. He had been framed, he said, and was the victim of a vendetta. Soon afterwards, West got an email saying: 'It's so fun watching people work so hard gathering all the evidence and then not being able to name me or catch me. You see, I always win. I always hold the trump card, and I will continue to make more movies. Next time you hear from me, it will be in a movie I'm producing that will have some humans, not just pussies.'

Scotland Yard were informed, but did not have the jurisdiction to do anything about it and Magnotta had by then disappeared.

Scary threat

Next, an anonymous post with a link appeared. It said: 'Hey, Deanna, brace yourself. This is a little frightening, Deanna, I don't want you to, you know, to worry too much, but ... go ahead and click this video.'

It showed the casino where Deanna Thompson worked. She was terrified that he was coming to kill her. But he wasn't.

On 25 May 2012, a video called 1 *Lunatic* 1 *Ice Pick* was posted. The title seems to have been inspired by 3 *Guys* 1 *Hammer*, a video made by three sadistic young men who murdered 21 people in and around Dnepropetrovsk in Ukraine, filming and posting footage of their crimes. 1 *Lunatic* 1 *Ice Pick* showed a naked man tied to a bed being repeatedly stabbed in a manner reminiscent of the opening scene of the film *Basic Instinct*. A poster of the film *Casablanca* is seen on the wall, so investigators concluded that the perpetrator was a movie buff. In the video, he goes on to dismember the body. Again, the police took no notice.

'Well, we told them this would happen and they didn't believe us,' said Green. 'And now we're looking at a dead person.'

There was a puppy in the video, putting the internet detectives in mind of the kittens. In the background the song 'True Faith' by New Order is playing. Luka had used that song before in some of the picture montages that he had posted on YouTube. The song also appears on the opening sequence of the film *American Psycho*.

Thompson and Green noticed a new picture of Luka in the video. He was in front of some steps. The trees were just coming into leaf, so it appeared to have been taken recently as it was then only late spring. They noticed that the pedestrian lights did not look like those in Toronto, but much more like those in Montreal.

Using Street View again, they found the steps were in McGill University in downtown Montreal. Green called the Montreal Police Department, to no avail.

Then, on 29 May, a blood-soaked box containing a human foot was delivered to the headquarters of the Conservative Party of Canada. With it was a poem that read:

'Roses are red.
Violets are blue.
Police will need...
dental file to identify you. Bitch.'

Another package containing a hand was intercepted in the mail addressed to the Liberal Party. Further body parts were sent to schools in Vancouver, while the head was dumped in a park. The torso was found by a janitor in a suitcase in an alley behind an apartment block at 5720 Decarie Street in Montreal. He had noticed maggots coming out of it. The arms, legs and head were missing and the trunk had been punctured many times.

Also in the bag were a yellow T-shirt, a wine bottle, a crumpled poster for the film *Casablanca*, the body of a puppy, a driver's licence from Ontario and a receipt from a pharmacy, the last two items with the name Luka Rocco Magnotta on them. The address on the receipt was Apartment 208, 5720 Decarie Street.

Scene of the crime

There was no one in the apartment, but there was the smell of chemicals. It had recently been cleaned. Checking the security cameras, the police found footage of a young man in his twenties, wearing a yellow T-shirt and making repeated trips out to the garbage early on the morning of 25 May. In the garbage, the police found a knife, a screwdriver that had been modified to look like an ice pick, some skin, and arms and legs, but no hands or feet.

On CCTV, the police also saw the victim – a 33-year-old Chinese student named Jun Lin – entering the building with Magnotta. Jun Lin's name was already on a missing persons report after an ex-boyfriend had grown concerned about his disappearance. DNA taken from a toothbrush found in his apartment matched the body. Magnotta seems to have picked him up on the website Craigslist.

Later, Magnotta was seen on CCTV leaving the building in the yellow T-shirt Jun Lin had been wearing on the way in. The sedative Oxazepam was found in Jun Lin's blood and in the wine bottle. Although Magnotta returned with rubber gloves and cleaning products, blood was found in his apartment using luminol, a chemical that glows blue on contact with an oxidizing agent such as blood. In the walk-in closet was written: 'If you don't like the reflection, don't look in the mirror. I don't care.'

But still no one knew where Magnotta was. The Montreal police called Green, who told them his guess was Paris. He figured that Luka had been planting movie clues in the videos. The film *Casablanca* ends with the lines: 'If that plane leaves the ground, and you're not with him, you'll regret it. Maybe not today, maybe not tomorrow, but soon and for the rest of your life.'

'But what about us?'

'We'll always have Paris.'

They contacted Montreal Airport to discover that Magnotta had bought a ticket to Paris. At Charles de Gaulle Airport, he was seen on CCTV, catching a cab. The taxi driver said he had dropped his passenger at the Novotel. Magnotta had a reservation there, but had not stayed. He had disappeared again. Luka was a fan of the movie *Catch Me If You Can*, where the protagonist repeatedly eludes the FBI. On 1 June 2009, he had posted the blog: 'Luka Magnotta: How to Disappear and Never Be Found.' It spelt out how to evade law enforcement.

The French police discovered that he had made a withdrawal from an ATM on the Place de Clichy, an area where he might find a fresh victim, so they continued searching for Magnotta in Paris. They found a rundown hotel where he had left the Mickey Mouse T-shirt he was wearing when he arrived at Charles de Gaulle. But it was soon found that he had already taken a bus to Berlin, where he was captured in an internet café reading material about himself online.

Flown back to Canada, Magnotta claimed that he had been forced to kill Jun Lin and the kittens by Emanuel 'Manny' Lopez, an escort client. Indeed, a third hand is seen in one of the kitten videos. However, there is no other evidence that Manny existed and it seems to have been a veiled reference to the film *Basic Instinct*. In the movie, Sharon Stone plays the ice pick-wielding Catherine Tramell, whose ex-boyfriend is said to have been Manny Vasquez. One of the numerous aliases Magnotta used was K. Tramell.

Magnotta pleaded not guilty of murder on the grounds of diminished responsibility. He was convicted and sentenced to life imprisonment, only eligible for parole after 25 years. He was also a suspect in another series of gay village homicides in Toronto, but the investigation was abandoned for lack of evidence. Besides, Magnotta was already in jail. He later married another inmate who he met online. His story is told in the Netflix series *Don't F**k With Cats*.

MARYBETH TINNING: MURDERING MOTHER

All nine of Marybeth Tinning's children died before they were five years old. She confessed to killing three of them, but was convicted of only one case of second-degree murder. No one has any clear idea of what motivated her to kill, unless this was the ultimate case of Munchausen syndrome by proxy, where a parent or care-giver covertly inflicts injury on a child to gain attention, praise or sympathy.

Marybeth Tinning, née Roe, was born in 1942 in the small town of Duanesburg ten miles south of Schenectady, upstate New York. She complained once of being an unwanted child and was shuffled between relatives in her early life, but there was a war on. She also complained of child abuse.

'My father hit me with a fly-swatter,' she said. 'Because he had arthritis and his hands were not of much use. And when he locked me in my room, I guess he thought I deserved it.'

This does not appear to have been an extreme form of discipline, given the standards of the time, but it was said that she tried to kill herself several times as a child.

She met her future husband Joe Tinning on a blind date in 1963. They married in 1965. Their first child, Barbara, was born in May 1967, their second, Joseph Jnr, in January 1970. The first to die was their third child Jennifer, born on 26 December 1971. She died on 3 January 1972 of haemorrhagic meningitis and multiple brain abscesses that had developed *in utero*.

As Jennifer never left hospital to be cared for by her mother, there was no indication of foul play. However, it had been pointed out that Marybeth's father died of a heart attack in October 1971. There is speculation that the two deaths, one closely following the other, pushed Marybeth over the edge. But there may have been a more sinister impulse at play.

'Jennifer looks to be the victim of a coat-hanger,' Dr Michael Baden, former chief medical examiner of the City of New York, said. 'Tinning had been trying to hasten her birth and only succeeded in introducing meningitis. The police theorized that she wanted to deliver the baby on Christmas Day, like Jesus. She thought her father, who had died while she was pregnant, would have been pleased.'

Seventeen days after the death of Jennifer, Marybeth took two-year-old Joseph Jnr to the emergency room of Ellis Hospital in Schenectady, saying he had had some type of seizure. He was kept in for observation, but doctors could find nothing wrong with him. However, a few hours after his release on 20 January, Marybeth brought the boy back, dead.

'He was taking a nap,' Marybeth told detectives in a later statement, 'it was close to his birthday and he had slept, taken a nap, slept unusually long. Unfortunately, I did not go in to check on him and, when I did, he appeared to be having respiratory problems which I did not cause.'

She had told the doctors that she had found him tangled in the sheets and his body had turned blue. His cause of death was listed as 'unknown' and no autopsy was performed.

Deaths two, three and four

Barely six weeks later, on 1 March 1972, Marybeth returned to the hospital with four-year-old Barbara, saying the little girl was suffering from convulsions. The doctors wanted the child to stay overnight, but Marybeth insisted on taking her home. She came back the next day with Barbara, who was by then unconscious. A few hours later, she died, possibly of a rare brain disease known as Reye's Syndrome.

Asked about Barbara's death 12 years later, Marybeth said: 'While we were sleeping, she called out to me and I went in and she was having a convulsion. I guess I don't even remember whether … I think maybe we just … I don't remember whether we took her by ambulance or whether we took her, but anyway we got there and they did whatever they did.'

Within 90 days, three of the Tinnings' children were dead. Days after Barbara's death, Marybeth asked the Schenectady Department of Social Services about becoming a foster parent. She got a job as a waitress and, that autumn, the Tinning family took in a foster child named Robert. They kept him until January 1973, when they took in another foster child named Linda. She was returned when Marybeth became pregnant again.

She gave birth to Timothy on 22 November 1973. Although he weighed just five pounds, Marybeth took him home two days later. She returned him to hospital after three weeks, dead. Marybeth told doctors she found him lifeless in his crib. Again, doctors found nothing medically wrong. Timothy seemed to be a normal baby. His death was listed officially as SIDS – Sudden Infant Death Syndrome, also known as cot death.

Marital problems

In 1974, things were not going well in the Tinnings' marriage. The couple argued over money and Joe Tinning turned up in hospital with a near-fatal overdose of barbiturates. Apparently, Marybeth had tried to poison him, though Joe said he had attempted suicide. Marybeth then admitted to stealing money from her sister-in-law Carol and agreed to see a psychiatrist, but she escaped from the mental hospital without her family knowing. She then reported to the police that her home had been burgled, though it was later concluded that she had staged the robbery herself.

Even so, the marriage stumbled on and Marybeth was soon pregnant again, but she told a co-worker not to tell anyone as 'God had told her to kill this one, too'.

On 30 March 1975, Marybeth gave birth to her fifth child, Nathan. He was barely five months old when Marybeth returned him to hospital, dead. She said she was driving her car with the baby in the front seat when he had suddenly stopped breathing. Again, there was no rational explanation. Doctors attributed his death to acute pulmonary oedema, or heart failure.

In 1978, Marybeth and her husband made arrangements to adopt a child. One would have thought that, given their track record, the agency might have had some misgivings. Perhaps they felt pity for the unlucky couple. However, that same year, Marybeth fell pregnant again. They decided to keep both children. In August, a boy, Michael, came from the adoption agency and, on 9 October, a daughter named Mary Frances was born.

On 20 January 1979, she was returned to the emergency room. Marybeth said she had had some kind of seizure. She was revived and the hospital recorded an 'aborted SIDS'. After being treated, she was sent home but returned on 20 February. Marybeth said she had found her in her cot unconscious. She had suffered a full cardiac arrest and was irretrievably brain-damaged. Two days later, she died after Marybeth agreed to turn the life support system off. Again, SIDS was recorded as the cause of death.

On 19 November that year, Marybeth gave birth to her seventh baby, Jonathan. In March 1980, he was returned to hospital unconscious. Revived, he was sent to Boston Hospital to be examined by experts who could find no medical reason as to why he had stopped breathing. He was sent home to his mother, but returned to hospital soon after. He died on 24 March 1980 after four weeks on life support in Albany.

On 2 March 1981, Marybeth showed up at her paediatrician's office with Michael, then two and a half years old. He was wrapped in a blanket and unconscious. Marybeth told the doctor that she could not wake Michael that morning and had no idea what was wrong. She described what happened later to police: 'When I went in in the morning to get him up and so we could go to the doctors, he was not, I mean he was responsive to a point but he was very limp and so on and so forth and so instead of calling an ambulance, I went from our house ... put him in the car, literally threw him in the car and went to St Clare's or I mean I went to Dr Mele's office and went in there and ... by the time one of the doctors ... I guess took me and they said that he died of viral pneumonia.'

When the doctor examined the boy, he was already dead. Later, a post-mortem found traces of pneumonia, but not enough to cause death. Since Michael was adopted, the theory that the deaths in the Tinning family might have had a genetic origin was discarded. There were other queries about Marybeth's odd behaviour. When she first realized that Michael was sick that morning, Marybeth could have easily come straight to the emergency room, which was just across the street from where she lived as she had done when the others had died. But, instead, she let hours pass until the doctors' office opened.

Birth of an eighth child

Now childless, Marybeth and Joe moved in with his parents in Duanesburg. They stayed for 11 months while Marybeth did a number of jobs, including working as a volunteer ambulance driver. They bought a trailer in Duanesburg that mysteriously caught fire. Marybeth was suspected. They moved back to Schenectady and Marybeth quit the ambulance brigade after a stolen first aid box was found near her home.

On 22 August 1985, Marybeth gave birth to her eighth child, Tami Lynne. Like all the other children in Marybeth's care, she was destined to have a short life. On 19 December, next-door neighbour, Cynthia Walter, a practical nurse, went shopping with Marybeth and later visited her home.

'I stayed for a few minutes and I wanted to hold Tami,' Cynthia said, 'but Marybeth asked me to give the baby back, so I handed her back and then I went home.'

Later that night, Cynthia received a frantic telephone call from Marybeth. 'Cynthia!' she said. 'Get over here right now!' When she went next door to see what was wrong, she found Tami Lynne lying on a changing table. 'She wasn't moving,' Walter testified. 'She was purple and I couldn't feel pulse or respiration. She was not breathing.'

She was rushed to the emergency room, where she was pronounced dead. Marybeth told Cynthia that Tami Lynne had got tangled in a blanket, though the following day she did not seem in any way upset. Knowing the family history, the hospital staff were also suspicious. Even Joe had misgivings by then.

'There were things to make me suspicious,' he said, 'but you have to trust your wife. She has her things to do and, as long as she gets them done, you don't ask no questions.'

That day, the Tinning family was visited by Betsy Mannix of Schenectady County's Department of Social Services and Bob Imfeld of the Schenectady Police Department, regarding the death of Tami Lynne. Blood was found on her pillow and a post-mortem determined that she had been suffocated.

Marybeth agreed to go to the police station where she was questioned and confessed to murdering Tami Lynne, Timothy and Nathan in a 36-page statement, which was disputed in court but allowed to stand. However, she denied killing any of the other children, although, with the exception of Jennifer, she had been alone with each child at the time they died.

Marybeth Tinning was only charged with the murder of Tami Lynne as there was forensic evidence to support the prosecution case. She had been indicted for the murders of Timothy and Nathan, but the charges were dropped.

The jury took three days to convict her of second-degree murder, clearing her of deliberately killing the child and finding her guilty of

Marybeth Tinning is led to the courtroom.

the lesser degree of homicide by her 'depraved indifference to human life'. Apparently, they were convinced of her guilt by the fact that she did not appear on the stand in her own defence. She was sentenced to 20 years to life.

At her first parole hearing in 2007, she was admonished for her lack of remorse. Appearing before the parole board again in 2009, she admitted killing Tami Lynne.

When she became eligible again in 2011, she explained: 'After the deaths of my other children … I just lost it, became a damaged worthless piece of person and when my daughter was young, in my state of mind at that time, I just believed that she was going to die also. So I just did it.'

She was released after a seventh attempt in 2018, aged 76. Her husband Joe was waiting for her. He had been visiting her every month for the 31 years she was in jail.

The question was still asked: why had it taken so long and so many young lives sacrificed before she was apprehended?

'Everyone did their jobs,' Schenectady police chief Richard E. Nelson told the press, 'but when you have a legitimate cause of death, where do you go from there?'

The New York Times offered vindication, saying: 'There were six autopsies, but never any signs of abuse. There were whispers and suspicions. But somehow no one – not the police, the coroner, doctors, social workers or neighbours, not even Mrs Tinning's husband – detected something evil in the strange pattern of deaths.'

LINDA HAZZARD:
FASTING SPECIALIST

Alternative medicine has always had its devotees and at the turn of the 20th century fasting was all the rage. In 1900, Dr Edward H. Dewey published *The No-Breakfast and the Fasting Cure*. He claimed that every disease that afflicts mankind was caused by 'more or less habitual eating in excess of the supply of gastric juices'.

Then in 1908, Linda Hazzard published *Fasting for the Cure of Disease*. But she took her methods a little far, using her 'beautiful treatment' to starve some 15 patients to death, while simultaneously robbing them of everything they owned. Nevertheless, she maintained: 'Death in the fast never results from deprivation of food, but is the inevitable consequence of vitality sapped to the last degree by organic imperfection.'

Born Linda Burfield in Carver County, Minnesota in 1867, she married at 18 and had two children, but left to study under Dewey and train as an osteopathic nurse in Minneapolis. It seems she killed her first patient while purporting to be a doctor in 1902, around the time her divorce became final. After the coroner determined that death was caused by starvation, he tried to have her prosecuted, but as she was not a licensed medical practitioner, she could not be held responsible. However, it was noted that the victim's valuable rings were missing.

She then married Samuel Christman Hazzard, a West Point graduate who had been drummed out of the military for embezzling army funds. A swindler, drunk and womanizer, he had been married twice before. Having failed to divorce one of his wives, he was sentenced to two years for bigamy.

Once he was released, they moved to Washington state to set up a sanatorium at Olalla, across the Puget Sound from Seattle, at a place called Wilderness Heights, which locals renamed 'Starvation Heights' after malnourished patients escaped and came into town begging for food.

Taking the cure

The first known fatality there was Daisy Maud Haglund, a 38-year-old Norwegian woman, whose parents were immigrants and the owners of Alki Point, the original settlement that became Seattle. Daisy died on 26 February 1908 after 50 days of fasting. She left a three-year-old son named Ivar, who would, ironically, go on to open the successful Seattle-based seafood restaurant chain that bears his name. However, the post-mortem determined she had stomach cancer and would have died anyway.

Other victims soon followed – Lenora and Ida Wilcox in 1908 and Blanche B. Tindall and Viola Heaton in 1909, while New Zealander Eugene Stanley Wakelin was reported to have committed suicide by shooting himself in the head while fasting under Hazzard's care. Hazzard had been appointed administer of his estate and drained it of funds. As the son of a British lord, it turned out he was not as rich as she expected him to be and she wired his lawyer asking for more money to pay the mortuary fees. Later, the British vice-consul in nearby Tacoma, Lucian Agassiz, speculated that he had been shot by the Hazzards, out of frustration at his poverty.

Mrs Maude Whitney succumbed in 1910. Civil engineer Earl Edward Erdman also took the cure in 1910 and died of starvation after three weeks. The *Seattle Daily Times* headline read: 'Woman "M.D." Kills Another Patient'. After his death, Erdman's diary was recovered. It recorded that his daily diet consisted of mashed soup or a cup of strained tomato broth, or else a small orange or two. He was in pain, slept badly, sweated profusely and suffered a fluctuating heartbeat. He died shortly after being hospitalized on 28 March while awaiting a blood transfusion.

The cure did not just consist of fasting. There were daily enemas, taking hours and using 24 pints of water, and patients were given scalding baths. Hazzard would also 'massage' her patients, repeatedly hitting her fist against their forehead and back, screaming 'eliminate', while they screamed in pain.

But patients kept on coming. Frank Southard, a partner in a law firm, and C.A. Harrison, publisher of *Alaska-Yukon* magazine, died under Hazzard's care in 1911, along with Ivan Flux, an Englishman who had come to America to buy a ranch and who had fasted for 53 days. During his treatment, Hazzard got control of his cash and property. When he died, his family was told he only had $70 to his name.

The authorities tried to step in when Lewis Ellsworth Rader, a former legislator and publisher of a magazine called *Sound Views*, began wasting away. He even owned the land Hazzard's sanatorium was built on. Hazzard treated him at the nearby Outlook Hotel in 1911, and health inspectors tried to convince him to leave but he refused. Hazzard spirited him away to a secret location where the authorities could not question him. At 5 ft 8 in tall, Rader weighed less than 100 pounds (seven stone or 45 kilograms) when he died.

The health director of Seattle had been powerless to step in as, due to a 'grandfather' loophole in state law, Hazzard was licensed as a doctor and her patients were willing participants. Given the fad for quackery, she had many loyal followers. She had a commanding personality and seemed to hypnotize her patients with her booming voice and flashing dark eyes. Her patients were afraid of her and couldn't bring themselves to disobey. There was talk that her command of spiritualism, theosophy and the occult gave her the ability to gull people into starving themselves to death. But the health director kept an eye on her. If she had treated any children, he said he would have stepped in.

Hypochondriac sisters

The case that forced the authorities to intervene was that of Claire and Dorothea 'Dora' Williamson, the orphaned daughters of a wealthy British army officer. They had been staying at the Empress Hotel in Victoria, British Columbia, when they saw an ad for Hazzard's book. When they ordered it, they received a brochure promoting Hazzard's Institute of Natural Therapeutics in Olalla. The two sisters were hypochondriacs and fancied they were suffering from a variety of minor ailments. Dora complained of swollen glands and rheumatic pains, while Claire thought she had a dropped uterus. They were already great believers in 'alternative medicine', and had given up both meat and corsets in an attempt to improve their health.

Imagining the institute was set in rolling countryside, they set off for Seattle to sign up for treatment without telling their family, who disapproved of their health faddism. Arriving in February 1911, they were told that the sanatorium in Olalla was not quite finished. Instead, Hazzard set them up in the Buena Vista apartment on Seattle's Capitol Hill, where she began feeding them a broth made from canned tomatoes, eight fluid ounces a day, no more, which was not enough to sustain life. They were given enemas in the bathtub, which was covered in canvas to support them when they fainted. Meanwhile, Dr Hazzard offered to store their jewellery and real-estate deeds in her safe.

By the time the Institute was ready to receive them in April, they were down to 70 pounds (five stone or 32 kilograms) and delirious, so ill that they had to be transported there in ambulances and a private launch. There was clearly something amiss with them. Their childhood nanny, Margaret Conway, was visiting family in Australia when she received a mysterious telegram on 30 April summoning her to visit them in Olalla.

Three weeks later, she set sail from Sydney, arriving in Vancouver on 1 June, where she was met by Sam Hazzard. On the way to Dr Hazzard's office in Seattle, he broke the bad news that Claire was dead. As Dr Hazzard explained it, the culprit was a course of drugs administered to Claire in childhood. These had shrunk her internal organs and caused cirrhosis of the liver. Claire, it seems, had been much too far gone for the 'beautiful treatment' to save her. Meanwhile, Dora had gone insane.

Margaret Conway was taken to the Butterworth mortuary to see Claire's embalmed corpse, but did not recognize her. The hands, shape of her face and colour of her hair seemed to belong to someone else. She weighed just 40 pounds (less than three stone or 18 kilograms).

Dora was a human skeleton weighing 50 pounds (three and a half stone or 22 kilograms) when Margaret got to visit her in Olalla. Living in a rough-hewn shack, there was so little flesh on her that it was painful to sit down. She begged Margaret to take her away, but changed her mind the next day, saying the cure was doing her a world of good.

Margaret stayed with Dora, hoping to convince her to leave. She also tried to sneak some rice or flour into her broth. Although the

Linda Hazzard.

patients were usually kept in isolation, they were allowed to mingle for the Fourth of July celebrations. Two of them approached Miss Conway, saying they were prisoners and begging her to get them out.

There was little Margaret could do. Dr Hazzard had been appointed the executor of Claire's considerable estate, as well as Dora's guardian for life. Dora had also signed over her power of attorney to Samuel Hazzard. Meanwhile, the Hazzards had helped themselves to Claire's clothes, household goods and an estimated $6,000 worth of diamonds, sapphires and other jewels. Margaret noticed that Dr Hazzard had the temerity to wear Claire's silk dressing gown and her favourite hat.

The 'serpent' takes the stand

As a lowly servant, Margaret did not feel that she could confront the Hazzards. Instead, she contacted the sisters' uncle John Herbert in Portland, Oregon, who came to Seattle and paid a thousand dollars to free Dora.

Herbert and Vice-Consul Agassiz set about investigating the goings-on at Hazzard's sanatorium. They drew up a list of at least 12 other wealthy patients who had died there. Their death certificates listed starvation as the cause of death, except the ones signed by Dr Hazzard.

Agassiz put pressure on the authorities in Kitsap County to prosecute Hazzard. They said they did not have the money, but the recovering Dora Williamson said she would pay. On 15 August 1911, Linda Hazzard was arrested and charged with murder. The headline of the *Tacoma Daily News* read: 'Officials Expect to Expose Starvation Atrocities: Dr. Hazzard Depicted as Fiend'.

Breaking the news of the dead heiress and the walking skeletons of Olalla, it was suggested that Dr Hazzard exercised some kind of black magic or mind control over her victims. The trial was held in the county court in Port Orchard, the county seat. One reporter cautioned people to avoid looking into the doctor's eyes in case she bewitched them. Another wrote: 'Many accounts of the family's action declare that the woman asserts an iron will over all with whom she is thrown in contact, her powers ranging from the weakened patient at the fasting sanatorium to the husband.'

Dr Hazzard said that she was being persecuted because she was a successful woman. This inspired suffragettes from across the Northwest and beyond. Hundreds flocked to the trial. One reporter counted 248 women in the line – the wives of navy officers, society women, even an odd consortium of female private detectives. Linda Hazzard played to the crowd.

'I am a great believer in women and will defend members of my sex at all times,' she told the press during a court recess. 'I would willingly place my fate in the hands of a jury of women at any time.'

She was up against men who opposed her natural cures and scorned her methods.

'I intend to get on the stand and show up that bunch,' she told reporters. 'They've been playing checkers, but it's my move. I'll show them a thing or two when I get on the stand.'

However, her lawyer kept her off the stand. Natural cures and her methods were not on trial. Rather it was alleged that Hazzard had killed Claire Williamson for money. Prosecuting attorney Thomas Stevenson called Hazzard a 'financial starvationist' and 'a serpent who trod sly and stealthy, yet with all her craft left a trail of slime'. He had a paper trail to prove it.

He showed that Hazzard had written Claire's will. The last entry of Claire's diary, written on the day she died, had also been forged by Linda Hazzard. It said that Claire wanted Hazzard to have her diamonds.

Other names in the natural health world offered their support during their trial. Henry S. Tanner, a doctor who fasted publicly for

40 days in New York City in 1880, agreed to testify in order to 'hold up the medical fraternity to the derision of the world'. He was denied the chance.

The judge also excluded patients who claimed that their treatment had been successful. However, John Ivar Haglund, widower of wife Daisy, testified that he had faith in Dr Hazzard. He had even taken their son to her for treatment. Nevertheless, she was found guilty of manslaughter and sentenced to two to 20 years' hard labour. An appeal failed. Meanwhile, it seems that Dr Hazzard managed to starve four more patients to death.

After she served two years in the state penitentiary at Walla Walla, she and her husband went to New Zealand where she styled herself physician, dietician and osteopath, and published another book. After making a lot of money, she returned to Olalla in 1920 where she built a dream sanatorium – one with an autopsy room in the basement – and where she continued her starvation treatment. Although for some unfathomable reason she had been pardoned by the state governor in 1916, her medical licence had been revoked, so she had to call it a 'school of health'.

It burnt down in 1935. By then, she was in her 60s. Feeling unwell, she subjected herself to her own fasting treatment and became her own last victim in 1938.

RICHARD COTTINGHAM: THE TORSO KILLER (THE NEW YORK RIPPER)

Also known as The Times Square Killer, Richard Cottingham seemed an unlikely serial killer. The 34-year-old married father-of-three had a respectable job and lived in suburban Bergen County, New Jersey, just over the George Washington Bridge from Manhattan. Neighbours described him as a doting father who always took his children out trick-or-treating at Halloween. Convicted of eight murders and known to have committed 11, he told a journalist 30 years after first being convicted that he had committed 80 to 100 'perfect murders' across the United States.

Born in 1946 in the Bronx, New York, he moved out to New Jersey with his family when he was two. He was a high-school athlete. The son of an insurance executive, he followed his father into the business. For 16 years, he had worked as a computer technician at Empire State Blue Cross-Blue Shield, a medical insurance company on Third

Avenue in midtown Manhattan, where he was considered a valued and dependable employee. By coincidence, he worked in the same office as the 'Dating Game Killer', Rodney Alcala, when he was on the run in 1969.

The following year, Cottingham married and the couple had two boys and a girl. His life seemed faultless until, in April 1980, his wife filed for divorce, alleging 'extreme cruelty' and his refusal to engage in marital sex since the birth of their third child in late 1976. She said that he stayed out all night, spending money that the couple could ill afford, and contended that Cottingham was an habitual patron of gay bars and homosexual bath-houses in Manhattan. In fact, he spent his time targeting prostitutes.

Cottingham would pick up his victims in bars or on the streets of Manhattan. Then he would buy them drinks or dinner and spike their glass with a date-rape drug. Once he got his semiconscious victim to his car, he would drive them across the Hudson River to New Jersey and take them to one of the cheap motels that lined the highways there. He would carry them in through the back door, then molest and torture them. The lucky ones would wake to find they had been raped and sodomized and covered with horrific wounds. They would either have been left on the floor of the motel room or dumped naked by a roadside with little memory of what had happened. The others would not wake at all.

Glassy-eyed zombie

Cottingham did not care whether his victims lived or died. He got his pleasure from torturing them. If they died before he was satisfied, he would continue abusing their corpse until he was done. Then he would abandon the victim like trash, whether she was alive or dead.

Despite claiming to have committed 'perfect murders', clues existed in a series of minor offences he was convicted of during his murder spree which seems to have begun in 1967. Two years later, he was fined $50 for drunk driving in New York City and another $50 in 1972 for shoplifting. The following year, he was arrested in New York City for robbery, sexual abuse and oral sex – then still considered sodomy – alleged by a prostitute and her pimp. The case was dropped when neither complainant turned up to court. Another case was dismissed in 1974, after a sex worker, who accused him of robbery and unlawful imprisonment, was again a no-show.

The NYPD did not realize that they had a serial killer on their hands until he moved the crime scene to Manhattan. On 2 December 1979, fire-fighters were called to a rundown Travel Inn motel near Times Square where one of the rooms was on fire. When they had doused the flames, they discovered the bodies of two women. Both were missing their heads and hands, which were never found.

The victims' clothes were found neatly folded in the bathtub with their then-fashionable platform shoes topping each pile. Except for blood soaked into the mattresses, the hotel room was remarkably free of bloodstains, fingerprints or useful evidence of any kind. The killer had taken the weapon he had used to kill them and dismembered the bodies with it. Aside from the mutilation, the bodies showed signs of horrific torture. There were cigarette burns, welts from beatings and bite marks around the breasts.

Cottingham had soaked their bodies with lighter fluid and set them ablaze to cover his tracks. While fleeing the hotel, he bumped into 23-year-old Peter Vronsky, Canadian historian and filmmaker, who was aiming to check in. He had shown up without a reservation and was told that a room would be available in half an hour, so he went to have a look around the hotel.

'As I waited at the elevator, I was mildly annoyed to see that it had stopped for what seemed an eternity on the top floor,' he said. 'Finally, the stalled elevator began to come down, and when the doors opened, presumably the jerk who had held the elevator on the upper floor got off. He almost walked over me like some kind of glassy-eyed zombie, looking right through me and brushing me aside as if I were not there. As he passed me by heading into the lobby, he lightly bumped my leg with a bag or a suitcase or something.'

After smelling the faint scent of burning emerging from the lift, Vronsky decided to find somewhere else to stay.

'All this gave me a bad vibe about the place (to say the least) and I left almost immediately to seek out another hotel without a glance backward,' he said. 'The next morning, I read in the newspapers that firemen responding to flames in one of the rooms of the hotel had discovered the corpses of two murdered women laid out on twin beds that had been set on fire. A fire-fighter had dragged one of the women out of the smoky room into the hallway and attempted to give her mouth-to-mouth resuscitation only to discover that she had no head or hands. At first, he thought it was a mannequin.'

A 15-year veteran of the NYFD, the fire-fighter said he nearly had to undergo trauma counselling afterwards. 'I've never come across something like that. I hope I never do again.'

At the time, Vronsky did not make any connection between the man he had bumped into and the killer. It only struck him when he saw Cottingham's picture in the newspaper after his arrest.

'Since then, I always assumed that when he stepped by me in the elevator that Sunday morning, he must have been carrying the severed heads and hands with him,' he said. 'I could not imagine him taking the risk of leaving two headless corpses unattended in the hotel room to go out and dump the heads and hands and then return to set fire to the room ... On the other hand, did he kill one woman and leave her body in the room, then go out to seek out another, or were they both alive together before he killed them? Cottingham never said.'

As the author of a bestselling series of true crime books, Vronsky went on to interview Cottingham in jail 40 years later, when the killer freely admitted the murders.

More victims

From X-rays, one of the victims was identified as Deedeh Goodarzi, a 22-year-old immigrant from Kuwait who was working as a prostitute to support her four-month-old baby. Cottingham was seen with her in a bar the night before. The other victim was never identified, though she appeared to be a teenager.

Although there was little to go on, detectives linked the killing to the case of teenage hooker, Helen Sikes, who had disappeared from Times Square in January 1979, ten months earlier. Her body turned up in Queens with her throat slashed so deeply that she was nearly decapitated. Her severed legs were found a block away, laid side by side as if still attached to the body.

On 5 May 1980, 19-year-old prostitute, Valerie Street, was found beaten and strangled, jammed under a bed at a Quality Inn in Hasbrouck Heights, New Jersey. She had been savagely beaten and her breasts had been gnawed so violently that one nipple was nearly severed. Around her mouth were traces of adhesive tape used to gag her. The tape had been taken away, but the handcuffs used to restrain her had been left. A fingerprint was found on the inner ratchet. It was the only fingerprint found that would eventually link Cottingham to the murders.

Detectives recalled that the body of 26-year-old radiologist, Mary Ann Carr, had been dumped by a chain-link fence near the parking lot of the same motel on 16 December 1977. She had been beaten with a blunt instrument. Her body was covered in bites and bruises, and there were cuts to her chest and legs. Her wrists showed marks from handcuffs and there were traces of adhesive tape around her mouth.

The connections were clear but took the police no nearer to finding the killer. Or so they thought. She had been abducted from an apartment complex in Little Ferry, New Jersey, where Cottingham had previously lived with his wife and where he would later leave an unconscious victim who would survive.

On 15 May, 25-year-old prostitute, Jean Reyner, was found in the Seville Hotel on 29th Street near Times Square. She had been stabbed to death. Her breasts had been hacked off and set down side by side on the headboard, then the room had been set on fire. Naturally, the NYPD saw parallels with the murders in the Travel Inn motel.

A week later, Cottingham was arrested. On 22 May 1980, he had picked up 18-year-old Leslie Ann O'Dell, who was soliciting on the corner of Lexington Avenue and 25th Street. She had arrived in New York on a bus from Washington State four days earlier and was quickly lured into prostitution by pimps at the bus station.

As a john, Cottingham appeared kind. He bought her drinks and told her about his job and his house in the suburbs. It was about 3am when he then offered to take her to the bus terminal in New Jersey, so she could escape the pimps in Manhattan and head home. Leslie eagerly accepted.

After crossing the George Washington Bridge, he bought her a steak at an all-night diner. She then agreed to have sex with him for $100. It was around dawn when they checked into the same Quality Inn in Hasbrouck Heights where he had left the mutilated body of Valerie Street 18 days earlier. No one at reception recognized Cottingham, but returning to the same venue once again would lead to his downfall.

Screams were heard

After renting a room, Cottingham drove around to the back of the motel and they entered through the rear door. Leaving the girl in the room, Cottingham returned to his car. He came back carrying a paper bag containing a bottle of whisky and an attaché case. It was then nearly 5am.

He offered to give her a massage and she rolled over on to her stomach. Straddling her, he pulled a knife from the attaché case and held it to her throat, then snapped a pair of handcuffs on her wrists. While Leslie tried to persuade Cottingham that this was unnecessary as she would do what he wanted anyway, he began torturing her, nearly biting off one of her nipples.

She later testified that he said: 'You have to take it. The other girls did, you have to take it too. You're a whore and you have to be punished.' This was a tacit admission that there had been other victims.

The motel staff heard a girl screaming and called the police. When they arrived, they caught a man trying to flee. Entering the room, they found a young woman handcuffed to the bed. She was in hysterics, saying she had been beaten, raped, sodomized and forced to give the

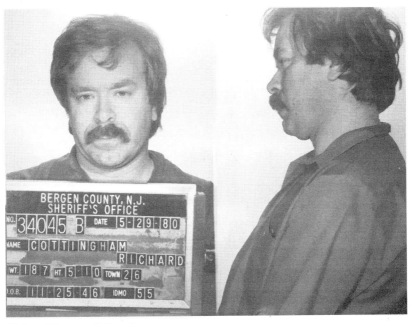

Richard Francis Cottingham.

man oral sex at knifepoint. He had stabbed her and bit almost right through her nipples.

Although Cottingham denied everything, it was found that he was carrying handcuffs, a leather gag, two slave collars, a switchblade, a replica pistol and a large number of pills.

In the basement of his home, the police found a trophy room where he kept some personal effects of his victims. He had kept the room locked after his wife instigated divorce proceedings.

In the case of Leslie Ann O'Dell, Cottingham was charged with kidnapping, attempted murder, aggravated assault, aggravated assault with a deadly weapon, three counts of aggravated sexual assault while armed for rape, sodomy and forced fellatio, possession of a weapon, possession of controlled dangerous substances, Secobarbital and Amobarbital or Tuinal, and possession of controlled dangerous substance, Diazepam or Valium. Conviction on those charges alone earned him 173 to 197 years in prison.

In the trials in New Jersey and New York that followed, he was also found guilty of four counts of second-degree murder. These brought him another 20 years, and 75 years to life.

In 2010, he pleaded guilty to the 1967 murder of 29-year-old housewife Nancy Vogel, whose naked body was found bound in her car. They had been neighbours and knew each other.

In 2021, he pleaded guilty to kidnapping, raping and drowning a pair of teenage girls in 1974. He also confessed to three murders of New Jersey schoolgirls in 1968 and 1969 in return for immunity from prosecution. Though he claimed to be responsible for up to 100 homicides, he has only been officially linked to 11.

'I have a problem with women,' he said.

RICHARD MARC EVONITZ: THE SPOTSYLVANIA SERIAL KILLER

After kidnapping, raping and murdering three young girls, Richard Marc Evonitz abducted and raped a fourth victim. But the 15-year-old was too clever for him. After enduring an horrendous sexual ordeal, she managed to escape. Evonitz then fled. While on the run, he confessed other crimes to his sister. Eventually, he was cornered. Surrounded by the police, he committed suicide.

Richard Marc Edward Evonitz was born in 1963 in Columbia, South Carolina. He was known as Marc to avoid confusion with his uncle who was also named Richard. Marc's parents separated soon after his birth, but re-united to have two daughters, Kristen and Jennifer, before finally divorcing in 1985. Throughout, the couple had extramarital affairs. Marc was made complicit, taking messages to his father's mistress.

His dad, Joseph Evonitz, had met his mother, Tess Ragin, while he was a soldier stationed at Fort Jackson in Columbia. She was a secretary on the base. They married in 1961, after he was discharged. They soon realized that the marriage had been a mistake but stayed together because Tess was pregnant.

There followed a series of menial jobs. Joe was usually fired for drunkenness or violent behaviour. He was no better at home. One Christmas Eve, he choked Tess to the point where she passed out. Marc was chased out of the house after spilling dog food. Kristen ended up in the emergency room with a gash to her head.

Jennifer said: 'We lived in a prison. He wanted us to make straight As. If we didn't, we were stupid. It was all about power and control. "You get an A or you'll get a beating."' Her father was a sadist, she said, who got pleasure out of making his family miserable.

The children said that Joe drowned Marc's dog in front of him. Joe denied that, saying the children were always adopting strays and he took one to the pound. Marc also maintained that Joe had tried to drown him in a paddling pool at the age of six when he had splashed water on some hamburgers during a cookout. Others say the incident happened in the bathtub. Joe said this was misinterpreted.

'One time when Marc was little, I gave him a bath,' he said. 'He kept yelling about the water going in his eyes, so I took a bunch of water and dumped it over his head.'

Joe wished he had never done it, but Marc never forgave or forgot and the incident seems to have played a crucial role in his development as a serial killer.

Off the rails

Living two doors away was a pretty young girl named Bonnie Lou Gower. She had a crush on Marc, but he was already going off the rails. A former Boy Scout and Little Leaguer, he began drinking and smoking at the age of 12 and starting using marijuana at 13, breaking into houses to support his habit. He was also making obscene phone calls to girls he knew from school, enjoying their discomfort in class the next day.

A clever child, Marc graduated from high school at 16. But for the next two years, he was stuck in dead-end jobs. He began writing bad cheques. When one for $350 cashed at K-Mart bounced, Joe had had enough. He gave Marc an ultimatum – get out of his house or join up.

In February 1984, Evonitz joined the US Navy and went to San Diego for training. He began writing to the underage Bonnie Lou. Meanwhile, his mother had joined CURE – Citizens United for the Rehabilitation of Errants. She began visiting Perry Deveaux, who was serving a life sentence for the rape and murder of a 23-year-old teacher, a crime he claimed he had not committed. After she divorced Joe, they married, but she divorced Deveaux 12 years later while he was still incarcerated after he finally confessed his guilt.

Following the break-up of his marriage, Joe hit rock bottom. He ended up living in a homeless shelter and working in a fast-food restaurant.

Training as a sonar technician in Jacksonville, Florida, Marc Evonitz was arrested in January 1987 for masturbating publicly in front of 15-year-old Kelli Ballard and her three-year-old sister. He pleaded no contest and was given three years' probation.

Childhood sweetheart

In August 1988, he married Bonnie Lou Gower, who was then 16, and moved to Portland, Maine, where he was stationed. He liked to blindfold her, tie her up and pretend to rape her for hours on end. They would also shave each other's private parts and he played her 'daddy'.

After he left the Navy in 1993, they moved to Spotsylvania, Virginia, where he got a job at a small engineering company. He was a hard worker, but he had a violent temper, was rude to customers and talked about women in a sexually degrading way. He filed his nails to a point and female employees gave him a wide berth. He was also known to be adept with weapons and, when discussing the Vietnam war, he said if he was captured by the Vietcong he would not be tortured.

'I'd stick a gun in my mouth and pull the trigger,' he insisted.

Things could only get worse. Carrying a .25 semi-automatic pistol, he crept into a house where there were two young girls home alone after school. He locked the 11-year-old in the bathroom, while he raped her 13-year-old sister. Though they gave a good description, he was not arrested, or even questioned.

Evonitz was increasingly impotent with Bonnie and could only achieve satisfaction with more extreme bondage and degradation. This was not to her taste and she began an internet affair with a man in California. When Evonitz discovered that he planned to come to Virginia to meet Bonnie; he said he would 'meet the guy with a baseball bat'. Instead, in August 1996, she went to California to see her new beau.

On 9 September, Evonitz left work early, saying he had a dentist's appointment, and abducted 16-year-old Sofia Silva from the front porch of her house, apparently without a struggle as her older sister was inside and was unaware that anything was amiss. Evonitz was seen driving home recklessly with loud music blaring. When a neighbour came round to admonish him, Evonitz slammed the door in his face. The next day, he called in sick.

Sofia's disappearance featured on *America's Most Wanted* on 14 September 1996. A month later, her body was found in Birchwood Creek, 30 miles away in King George County. Her pubic hair had been shaved and her body was bound using knots Evonitz had learned in the Navy.

By then, Bonnie had returned from California. The marriage was irretrievably over and she started packing to move out. Evonitz began working out. On the way home from the gym one day, he told a neighbour that a young college girl had flirted with him. The neighbour said he should go with someone his own age. Evonitz replied: 'But I like them young.'

After Bonnie had left, Evonitz could no longer afford to pay the bills and, in 1997, he went bankrupt. On 1 May, he abducted 15-year-old Kristin Lisk and her 12-year-old sister Kati Lisk from their front yard in Spotsylvania. A week later, their bodies were found 35 miles away in the stagnant water of the South Anna River in Hanover County. Again, their pubic hair had been shaved and their lungs were filled with bath water, not the putrid water of the slow-moving river.

Chance meeting

In 1999, Evonitz, then 36, met 17-year-old Hope Marie Crowley when she was waiting tables at Aunt Sarah's Pancake House in Massaponax. He was having breakfast there with his mother and sister. When he flirted with Hope, his sister encouraged her to go out with him.

'We just clicked,' said Hope after his death. 'There were a lot of things about him that are very much like me, too.'

When Hope turned 18, she moved to Columbia, South Carolina, where Evonitz was living with his sister Kristen. They married and got their own apartment. Again, he insisted on shaving her pudendum, tied her up and played 'daddy'.

Spotsylvania Sheriff Howard Smith said: 'He'd ask her to dress up like a young girl and then he would actually force his way into their apartment and act like he was raping her.'

Young and naïve, Hope found this perfectly normal.

'When the FBI started talking to me about bondage and all that sort of stuff, they acted like it was such atrocious behaviour,' she said later. 'Our sex life was not extreme in any sense of the word. People do that sort of thing all the time.'

Detectives were puzzled why Evonitz ceased being a predator

between 1987 and 1996, and again between 1997 and 2002. This appears to be because his fantasies were being indulged at home. However, once his young wife grew into a full-grown woman, he went out searching for younger prey.

Nightmare ordeal

On 23 June, Hope flew to Orlando, Florida, with her mother-in-law Tess and Kristen's seven-year-old son to visit Disney World and stay with sister-in-law Jennifer. The following day, Evonitz abducted 15-year-old Kara Robinson Chamberlain from a friend's yard. He pretended to be selling magazines, then pulled a gun and forced her into his car.

'He put me in a plastic container in the back seat and stopped after ten or 15 minutes and put handcuffs on me,' she said. He also put a rope around her neck and stuffed paper towels in her mouth.

Arriving at his home, he took the container into the house. He told her that he would not hurt her if she did as she was told, then he raped her. He forced her to have a bath and they played house, with him washing the dishes, wiping down the counters and vacuuming, while she volunteered to sweep the floor to gain his trust.

'But when it came time for bed, he tied me up again,' she said.

Kara was handcuffed and her legs were shackled, and her arms and feet tied with rope to a wooden frame designed to be used for restraint. When she heard Evonitz snoring, she managed to untie the rope and sneaked out of the house, still in her handcuffs and leg shackles. The nightmare had lasted 18 hours.

Although the police had been treating Kara's disappearance as a teenage runaway, her reappearance quickly disabused them of that notion. Evonitz was a wanted man and Kristen called her mother at Disney World.

'Marc's all over the news,' she said. 'Police are looking for him. He kidnapped a girl at gunpoint and held her in the apartment.'

'That's ridiculous,' her mother said. 'Why are you saying this to me? It can't be true.'

Kristen repeated the message three times. She knew what she was talking about. Earlier, she had met her brother in a hotel in Orangeburg and he had confessed.

The following day, police said, one of Evonitz's relatives called him from the police station in Columbia to warn him that the police were on the way to Orangeburg to arrest him. By the time police arrived at the Days Inn where he was staying, Evonitz was gone.

They traced him to Sarasota, Florida. On 27 June, they surrounded him and urged him to surrender peacefully. He would not drop the pistol in his hand, so they released a police dog that bit him several times. Evonitz then turned the gun on himself. He was declared dead at 10.52pm.

'Picking me, that was the greatest mistake of his life,' Kara said, appearing on *America's Most Wanted*. She was only sorry that he was dead.

'I wanted him to go to trial and let him see me again and know I was his downfall,' she said.

When police interviewed his widow, Hope Evonitz, she refused to believe them and blamed Kara for what happened. Even if Marc did it, Hope said, it didn't matter to her. She still loved him.

'I don't look at him as a horrible person for what he did,' she said recently. 'I think that he just acted out on things that other people think of.'

But she was not entirely blind to what drove him.

'I'd seen glimpses of his dark side,' she said later. 'It was really my intuition; I'd wonder if he'd done something. He would get quiet and dark.'

His mother Tess also recognized a sense of inadequacy in her son, a feeling of inferiority. Despite all the bragging he did about how smart he was and his successes at work, she knew that Evonitz considered himself a failure. The assaults by his father had taken their toll, she said.

The murders of Sofia Silva and Kristin and Kati Lisk were also cleared up when analysis showed that hair from Marc Evonitz matched hairs found on the bodies of all three girls. Acrylic fibres from the blue 'furry' handcuffs he owned were found on all three girls' bodies. A palm print and fingerprints matching Kristen Lisk's were also found inside the trunk of Evonitz's car. This was described by one forensic scientist as a 'miracle' because they had been discovered five years after the abduction.

For five years, the task force assigned to the murders had chased more than 12,000 tips. More than 10,000 pieces of evidence, including human and animal hairs, fibres and tyre treads, had been examined, Spotsylvania county sheriff Ronald Knight said. DNA gathered from the crime scene was compared with 1.2 million samples in law enforcement databases and evidence was compared with clues from 45,000 other unsolved cases.

CHARLES ALBRIGHT: THE EYEBALL KILLER

On 13 December 1990, the semi-naked body of 33-year-old Mary Lou Pratt, a well-known hooker, was found on the 8800 block of Beckleyview in the Oak Cliff district of Dallas, a neighbourhood known for drugs and prostitution. She was wearing only a T-shirt and a bra, which had been pulled up to expose her breasts, and she had been shot in the back of the head with a .44 handgun. When an autopsy was performed, the medical examiner found that she had been badly beaten and her eyes had been removed with almost surgical precision, leaving barely a mark on the surrounding tissue. They had not been gouged out in a fight, but had seemingly been taken as a bizarre memento. Or something stranger might be at work.

From the birth of photography until well into the 20th century, forensic scientists seriously investigated the pseudoscience of optography. This was the belief that the last thing a dead person saw was imprinted on their retina. If this optogram could be retrieved in the case of a murder victim, it would be possible to obtain an image of the murderer. It was a technique used, unsuccessfully, in the search for Jack the Ripper and, in earlier times, murderers had been known to remove the eyeballs of their victims just in case.

Otherwise, there were few leads to go on, but it was rumoured that Mary Lou and another prostitute named Susan Beth Peterson had stolen goods from the warehouse of a customer who might have had a grudge against them. However, detectives were unable to find out who he was and the trail of The Eyeball Killer went cold.

Around the same time, another prostitute named Veronica reported that a man had raped her and tried to kill her. She had managed to escape but was left with a vicious head wound. On 15 December, she was seen in a light-blue truck. Figuring that the driver might be the man who had attacked her, the police stopped the vehicle. But Veronica insisted that the man had actually rescued her from her attacker. He called himself 'SpeeDee' and his driver's licence gave his address as Eldorado Avenue nearby. He said he lived there with his wife, Dixie, and maintained that he and Veronica were just friends.

On 10 February 1991, the semi-nude body of 27-year-old Susan Peterson was found on the same street. Her top had been pulled up to reveal her breasts in the same way that Mary Lou Pratt's had been. She too had been shot – once in the back of the head, once in the top of the head and once more in the left breast with the bullet entering her heart. Again, her eyes had been removed. Two days before she died, she had told patrol officers that she might know who Mary Lou's killer was. Veronica then claimed that she had actually witnessed Pratt's murder, but she was a known liar.

Pratt and Peterson were white, but on 18 March the body of 41-year-old, part-time prostitute, Shirley Williams, an African-American, was found. Williams had been shot in the top of the head and through the face. Once again, her eyes had been removed, but this time more roughly and the broken tip of an X-Acto precision knife was found.

Shirley's face had been slashed. She was badly bruised and her nose was broken.

That night, it appears, she had been getting high on drugs with friends before going out. It had been raining, so she had put on a yellow raincoat. She was last seen getting into a car. Earlier, she had told her daughter that she would be home that night, but she did not return. In none of these three cases were any fingerprints or semen found. However, among Williams's pubic hairs, the hair of a Caucasian man was found and the ballistics lab determined that the same gun had been used to kill Williams and Pratt.

The search for SpeeDee

Desperate for a lead, the police thought they would follow up on SpeeDee. The address on his driver's licence, they discovered, was a property registered in the name of Fred Albright. But he was dead.

A woman then came forward with her suspicions. She knew Charles Albright, Fred's son. He had told her that he was a professional con man and had showered her with gifts. Although he was married, he moved her into a love nest, but she had become increasingly disturbed by his behaviour, particularly his obsession with eyes and knives. Eventually, she had moved out and moved on. She also said that Albright had known Mary Lou Pratt.

Veronica and another prostitute who had escaped by spraying an attacker with Mace were shown a photograph of Albright. Both recognized him as the man who had attacked them. On the night of 22 March, the police went to Albright's house on Eldorado and arrested him for attempted murder and assault. They also took in his wife Dixie. But SpeeDee did not live there. It was only the address on his driver's licence.

In Albright's home, the police found red condoms – one had been found by Shirley Williams's body. They also found some X-Acto knives like the one used to remove the eyeballs of at least one of the victims. Albright denied having a gun, but the police found a .44 Smith & Wesson revolver.

Dixie was shocked that her husband was wanted in connection with such horrendous crimes and provided him with an alibi. On the nights concerned, she said, he had been at home in bed with her, though he did have an early morning paper round. She did not know why he had condoms as she had passed her menopause. Nor did she know he already had a criminal record, including a conviction for sexual assault.

Albright denied knowing anything about the murders, nor did he consort with prostitutes, he said. SpeeDee, it turned out, was one of Albright's tenants, but he denied that Albright was the man he had rescued Veronica from.

But detectives kept digging. It seemed that Albright had been seeing prostitutes behind his wife's back, though he had once said he hated prostitutes and wanted to kill them. He had a fierce temper and, apart from his paper round, he lived off Dixie, who was a widow. Clearly, he was a manipulative, intelligent charmer.

Obsession with eyes

Born on 10 August 1933, Charles Albright had been adopted as a child. When he got his first gun, he would kill small animals and stuff them. He told a doting adoptive mother that he wanted to be a taxidermist. She encouraged him, but would not let him complete his taxidermy projects, making him leave his stuffed animals without eyes because the glass eyes in the local taxidermy shop were too expensive.

Although Albright graduated from high school with good grades, he got into North Texas State University by underhand means, using forgery. He was then arrested for stealing some money, a rifle and two handguns and was sentenced to a year in jail. Released, he continued his education.

At Arkansas State Teachers' College, he cheated in exams and bragged about his sexual prowess. When a flatmate broke up with a girl with distinctive almond eyes, he cut the eyes out of her photograph and pasted them on the photograph of his chum's new girlfriend. Other pictures of eyes were stuck on the ceiling and in the bathroom of their apartment.

Before graduating, he was expelled from college for stealing, so he forged a bachelor's and master's degree. Found out, he was sacked from his teaching job. He then married his college girlfriend and they had a daughter, but the marriage soon fell apart and they divorced.

Caught stealing again, he was sentenced to two years, but served only six months. Visiting friends, he was accused of molesting their nine-year-old daughter. He claimed he was innocent, but pleaded guilty to avoid the hassle of having to defend himself, he said, and escaped with probation. His probation officer said that he lied so readily that he often convinced himself that he was telling the truth.

Having inherited property from his father, he squandered money on prostitutes. He also gave them things he stole. After he met Dixie in Arkansas in 1985, she invited him to come and live with her. He accepted and let her pay all the bills. His only contribution came from his paper round, which was largely an excuse to get out of the house to visit hookers.

Off the road

Despite his shady background, the case against him began unravelling. The .44 Magnum found in his house was not the one used to kill Mary Pratt and Shirley Williams. No blood or any other evidence of murder was found in his house, and Dixie produced garage bills showing that their car was off the road when the first two murders occurred.

A stash of pornographic material was found in SpeeDee's house. Albright had a key and, it seems, used the place when SpeeDee was away. Hairs on blankets from Albright's truck and in his vacuum cleaner came from an African-American, but there were not enough of these to identify them as coming from Shirley Williams, given the DNA technology at the time. Even so, on 26 March 1991, capital charges were brought against Albright for the murders of Mary Pratt, Susan Peterson and Shirley Williams.

Then Mary Beth, a prostitute in custody, told the police that, on the night Mary Pratt had been killed, a man had forced her into a car at knifepoint. He drove her out to a field, threw her to the ground and kept punching her. Then he opened a case, got out a knife and slashed open her blouse. He discarded the blade. While he searched for another one, she passed out. When she came round, he was gone.

Interviewing other prostitutes in the area, the police came across a girl called Tina, who had beautiful eyes and said Albright had once been a regular client, but she dropped him when he got rough. On the night Shirley Williams died, Albright had driven past the two of them. Tina had got into another car, so did not see if Albright picked Shirley up. But when she got back, Shirley was gone. She took the police to a field where Albright used to take her. There, they found a yellow raincoat like the one Shirley had been wearing on the night she disappeared. It had blood on it.

Willie Upshaw, who was serving time for the illegal possession of a firearm, said that Albright had another .44 which the police had not found. He had bought it using his father's name. Upshaw had also been with Albright the day his car had broken down and said that he did have a car on the night Shirley Williams was killed.

A grand jury was called. They reduced the capital charges to murder in the second degree, taking the death penalty off the table. The district attorney then decided only to go ahead with the case of Shirley Williams.

The trial began on 2 December 1991, with the judge ruling that the other cases could be brought up in court to show a pattern of behaviour. The prosecution maintained that Albright was enraged after Mary Pratt and another prostitute had ripped him off. Another prostitute testified that she had been with Susan Peterson when Albright picked them up and beat them savagely.

However, the yellow raincoat the police had found had gone missing. Neighbours testified that Albright did not have a car at the time of the murder. Upshaw changed his story and Veronica appeared for the defence.

The case depended on the forensics and the scientific evidence concerning the hair, but it was enough for the jury to convict Charles Albright for the murder of Shirley Williams. The verdict was not reversed on appeal. He was sentenced to life imprisonment and died in the John Montford Psychiatric Unit in Lubbock, Texas on 22 August 2020, aged 87. To the end, he was unapologetic.

'You won't find any woman who'll say anything other than that I was always a perfect gentleman in their presence,' he said. 'I was always trying to do things for women. I would take their pictures. I would paint their portraits. I would give them little presents. I was always open for a lasting relationship.'

He maintained his innocence to the end. And some believed him.

'Look, I've known Charlie for 30 years,' one Albright friend, a retired Baptist minister, told *Texas Monthly*. 'In all that time, I think I would have seen his dark side slip out at least once. Believe me, if he really was a psychotic killer, he couldn't have kept it a secret all this time, could he?'

But then some people can see no evil. What's more, the missing eyeballs were never found.

'I don't think anybody would want to keep eyeballs,' Albright said.

'That would be the last thing I would want to keep out of a body. It would be a hand or a whole head, maybe, if you were a sick artist and you thought the woman was fabulous. You might not want to see that beauty go to waste.'

If Albright was innocent, perhaps the retina of those eyeballs did have the real murderer's image imprinted on them.

JOSEPH JAMES DEANGELO: THE GOLDEN STATE KILLER

While 'The Night Stalker' Richard Ramirez, who had terrorized southern California in 1985, languished on death row in San Quentin, Joseph James DeAngelo, aka 'The Original Night Stalker', remained at large for another 33 years. He had started out as the 'Visalia Ransacker' in 1973. Adding rape to his repertoire, he become the 'East Area Rapist' or 'East Side Rapist' or 'East Bay Rapist'.

Then came the killings as the 'Orange Coast Serial Killer' or the 'Creek Bed Killer' or the 'Diamond Knot Killer'. He became 'The Original Night Stalker' because his MO closely resembled Ramirez's, raping and killing his victims in their own homes. But then he went on to become 'The Golden State Killer' in 2013, only to be caught in 2018, after decades of raping and killing, thanks to an open-source DNA website.

The killer's training ground was the city of Visalia in California's San Joaquin Valley and nearby Exeter, where DeAngelo was a policeman at the time, often responding to crimes he had committed. In the mid-1970s, he committed more than 100 burglaries in the area, rummaging through drawers, strewing items around his victim's house, re-arranging things and stealing small, insignificant items. He would often ignore banknotes and high-value objects in favour of coins and trading stamps, indulging in meaningless acts of vandalism and scattering women's underwear over the floor. Wearing gloves, he'd leave no fingerprints and, undetected, a burglar with his MO could commit up to 12 break-ins a day.

Things got more serious when, on 11 September 1975, he broke into the house of Claude Snelling at 12.15am and tried to abduct his 16-year-old daughter Elizabeth. Running to her rescue, Snelling was shot twice in the chest with a .38-calibre handgun. The masked intruder let Elizabeth Snelling go and fled, leaving behind a stolen bicycle. Claude Snelling staggered back into the house and died. He had been a professor at the College of the Sequoias, where DeAngelo had trained to be a police officer. A reward of $4,000 was offered, but the murder remained unsolved until DeAngelo admitted to it in 2018.

Masked man with a gun

With a killer on the loose, the police redoubled their interest. On the evening of 12 December 1975, they were staging a stakeout in an avenue the Ransacker was thought to frequent. A masked man was seen entering the backyard of a house. Confronting him, Detective William McGowen fired a warning shot. The man went to pull off his mask as if to surrender. Then, suddenly, he vaulted the garden fence, pulled a gun and shot McGowen. As other officers ran to McGowen's aid, the prowler made off, dropping his plunder – again, coins and trading stamps – and leaving the tracks of tennis shoes.

In August 1979, DeAngelo quit the burglary unit at Exeter and moved to Auburn, a district of Sacramento. The crime spate followed him and the so-called Cordova Cat Burglar began a series of burglaries in the suburbs of Carmichael, Citrus Heights and Rancho Cordova. Breaking into one house, he was confronted by a woman brandishing a gun. A shot was fired and he fled. She gave a description that later matched that of the East Side Rapist who would soon stalk the East Area of the city.

As the East Side, or East Area, Rapist, DeAngelo committed 50 rapes in California between 1976 and 1986 and killed at least 12. His first 15 victims in late 1976 and early 1977 were almost all women at home alone – though one attack was in a parking lot. In one case, he

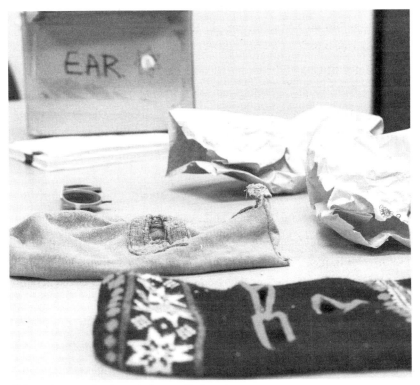

Ski masks worn by Joseph James DeAngelo.

seems to have waited until the woman's husband left the house before he attacked.

Other victims included a 16-year-old girl, who was raped, and an 18-year-old youth in East Sacramento, who was shot in the stomach when he confronted and chased the prowler. The perpetrator escaped even though a police cordon was thrown around the neighbourhood.

The pattern of attacks

At the beginning of November 1976, a reward of $2,500 was offered for information leading to his arrest. That was later increased to $25,000, with a local dentist adding $10,000 to the $15,000 offered by the *Sacramento Bee*'s Secret Witness programme.

The *Bee* said that the perpetrator entered houses though a window like a cat-burglar and gave a description. He was white with a pale complexion, between 5 ft 8 and 6 ft tall, 23 to 35 years old, with a medium build and dark hair that hung over his ears and collar.

Later descriptions make him younger – between 18 and 25 – and of a slighter build. Though muscular, it was thought he weighed 140 to 180 pounds (10 to 13 stone or 64 to 82 kilograms) and was extremely agile.

'He had worn a mask, but descriptions are vague as to what kind,' the newspaper said. He also wore gloves, so left no fingerprints. 'He has worn military-type boots and black tennis shoes. His weapons have included a revolver, knife, a stick and a club. He has cut and beat his victims, but none severely.'

The *Bee* added chillingly: 'He frequently commits repeated attacks on individual victims over a period of three hours.'

This was a serial killer waiting to happen.

After April 1977, he began attacking couples, too, targeting 'low-risk' victims – lawyers, medical professionals, computer programmers – people without a great deal of physical strength who were unlikely to fight back. He stalked upper-middle-class neighbourhoods looking for victims who lived in single-storey homes. Breaking in late at night, he then pulled a handgun. Always well-prepared, he brought pre-cut lengths of rope and cord with him to bind his victims.

He varied his pattern slightly when teenagers were involved. In one case, he raped two sisters who were at home alone together. He also molested a 13-year-old girl while her mother was tied up, and raped a 15-year-old babysitter in front of her eight-year-old ward.

Detailed planning

It was noted that, near the houses where the attacks took place, there was usually a drainage ditch, vacant field, new construction, park area or one of the levees of the American River that runs through Sacramento, so he could make his approach and exit with little chance of being spotted. He entered a residence at night through an unlocked sliding glass door or window, although he pried open doors and windows if necessary. Once inside, he threatened the victim with a knife, gun or club. He tied them up with the ligatures – often shoelaces – he brought with him. Then he used electrical tape and strips of towelling he found in the house to further bind, gag and blindfold his victims. He usually cut telephone wires and covered a lamp to dim the lighting.

When attacking a couple, he would often force the man to lie on the floor with perfume bottles or plates stacked on top of him while he raped the female, threatening to kill them both if the man moved enough to tip the bottles on to the floor or rattle the dishes.

He spent between one and three hours in the house, sexually assaulting the victim several times. In between the assaults, he would wander about the house eating and drinking. Sometimes he would even go out. Beverage containers were found outside where the suspect apparently stood, watching for anyone approaching the house.

He would also look through photograph albums and lingerie drawers, stealing small items of costume jewellery, class rings, ear-rings and items of little value.

Because of the way he moved in and out of the house, the victims rarely knew when the attacker had left the premises. It would usually take them between 30 minutes and an hour before they were able to free themselves. Sometimes, they would be unable to do so and would have to wait for assistance.

Upping the stakes

On 7 May 1977, while attacking a couple in Carmichael, the rapist said that he would kill his next two victims. This was what the police had long feared. But he stayed his hand when he attacked a couple in the South Area of Sacramento, near the office of the dentist who had put up the $10,000 reward. Gun and lock sales soared.

It became plain to the police that the attacker had detailed knowledge of his victims. He knew that the father of one victim was out of town for the weekend and that another's father was on vacation. The rapist knew families' habits and work hours. He caught one victim when her sister was at friends' and her parents were at a Christmas Party; another when her parents were out; another when her parents were away for the weekend.

He knew the schedule of spouses, catching one lone woman when her husband had relocated to the Bay Area where she was to follow; another when her husband was on a business trip; another when her husband had just left for work; and a fourth when her husband had started on the night shift just two days before the attack. And he attacked one woman who was separated from her husband while her son was visiting his father.

His knowledge could be thorough. He knew the purse of one victim was in her car. In another attack, he knew where the garage door-opener was. In one particular case, the outside lights were on a timer and he knew how to turn them off.

Explaining one attack, the assailant later said that he had seen the victim at Mather Officer's Club and knew her husband was a captain in the Air Force. However, his intelligence was not always 100 per cent accurate. In one case, he mentioned that his victim attended American River College. She did not, but a neighbour, who strongly resembled the victim, had attended the college. It was thought that the offender had been in the other woman's home as well, though he had not attacked the occupant.

It was not clear how he got his information unless it was from close observation of his intended victims. Footprints from herringbone-pattern tennis shoes were discovered under the bathroom window in numerous cases where he could have overheard conversations. He

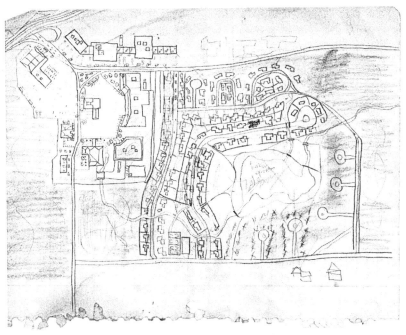

A 'punishment' map drawn up by the East Area Rapist.

also returned to the same area repeatedly, making maximum use of the intelligence he had already gathered.

The police almost caught the attacker on 12 December 1977, when officers spotted a man wearing a ski mask on a stolen bicycle on the Watt Avenue bridge in the East Area of Sacramento. He was seen again two hours later by city patrolmen near an apartment complex on La Riviera Drive near Watt, a place where he had struck three times before. But still he eluded them.

The first killings

The longer his career as a serial rapist got, the more violent, cruel, abusive and threatening he became. He made nine more increasingly savage attacks before he finally lived up to his word and became a killer.

On 2 February 1978, he shot dead Brian K. Maggiore, a sergeant at Rancho Cordova Air Force Base, and his wife of 18 months, Katie. They confronted a prowler when walking their dog down a quiet residential street. Katie was shot in the head. Brian was pursued into the backyard of a home on La Alegria Drive where he was shot fatally in the chest. The suspect was spotted by residents as he fled the scene. He was described as white, in his mid-twenties, 6 ft to 6 ft 2 in tall, with dark hair and wearing a brown leather coat with a large stain on the back, dark pants and shoes. He might have been with an accomplice, witnesses said. A pair of shoelaces was found at the crime scene. Two weeks later, composite drawings of the suspect were published in the *Sacramento Bee*. After that, the East Area Rapist never struck in the Sacramento area again.

The perpetrator moved on to the surrounding area – Stockton, Modesto, Danville, Fremont, Concord, San Ramon, Davis and Walnut Creek. A student at the University of California, Davis was attacked in her apartment with extreme physical violence on 7 June 1978. A month later, another woman was attacked in Davis and raped in front of her two sons. And on 25 June 1979, a 13-year-old girl was attacked while her parents were in another room asleep.

On 1 October 1979, a man in a ski mask entered the home of a couple in Goleta, Santa Barbara County. They were awakened, a flashlight shining in their eyes. The woman was ordered to tie up her boyfriend with pre-cut lengths of cord that the attacker had brought with him. While the masked intruder ransacked the house supposedly looking for money, the woman managed to get out of the house and scream for help. The intruder pulled her back inside. While he was doing this, the man escaped into the backyard. While the intruder pursued the man, the woman escaped again, running into the arms of a neighbour who had been alerted by her screams. Having lost control of the situation, the intruder fled. He was seen escaping on a bicycle down a creek bed.

After this couple had thwarted him, the attacker turned to killing in earnest. Two months later, on 30 December 1979, another couple were attacked a few blocks away. Dr Robert Offerman and Alexandria Manning were found shot dead. Both of them were tied up and Manning had been raped. Examination of the crime scene led detectives to believe that Offerman had managed to loosen his bindings and lunge at the intruder before he was shot and killed. Neighbours who heard the gunshots thought that they were firecrackers.

On 13 March 1980, the Stalker moved just 35 miles down the coast to Ventura, where he killed Lyman and Charlene Smith. Charlene was raped and both were bludgeoned to death with a log from their fireplace. The Smiths were found still bound in their bedroom by their 12-year-old son. Their wrists and ankles had been tied with drapery cord and an ornate 'Chinese knot' was used on their wrists. Although there were similarities to the attacks in Goleta, the Smiths' murder was not immediately linked to the others. Ventura detectives suspected Joe Alsip, a former business partner of Lyman Smith, who was later exonerated.

Next couple to die

Keith and Patrice Harrington were the next victims. They were also bludgeoned to death in their home in Dana Point on 19 August, as the killer moved south of Los Angeles for the first time. This time, the murderer untied his victims before escaping, but left some cord lying on the bed. He took the murder weapon with him when he left. A single burnt match was found in the home by investigators. Patrice had been brutally raped before her death. Law enforcement agencies theorized that the male victims had been bludgeoned to death first. Then the terrified female victims were raped before they too were killed by bludgeoning.

Next, the killer attacked 28-year-old Manuela Witthuhn on 5 January 1981, while her husband was in the hospital ill. Her killer entered her home in Irvine, Orange County. He raped her and beat her to death, then disappeared, taking with him the bindings along with the murder weapon and, curiously, Witthuhn's answering machine, a lamp and a crystal curio. As in the Smiths' case, burnt matches were found in Witthuhn's home.

Cheri Domingo and Gregory Sanchez were killed on 27 July 1981 back in Goleta, just half a mile from the scene of the Offerman–Manning murders. Sanchez had been shot once in the face and then bludgeoned to death. Cheri Domingo was simply bludgeoned. Again, the killer took the ligatures he had used to bind his victims and the murder weapon with him. The attacker's familiarity with the area led police to believe he lived near the San Jose Creek.

Then for five years, the killer lay low. He struck one last time on 4 May 1986, killing Janelle Lisa Cruz only a mile from Witthuhn's home in Irvine. Her family was away on vacation in Mexico at the time. Cruz was raped and beaten to death like the previous victims. The murder weapon was thought to be a pipe wrench that was found to be missing from her home. Cruz was attacked soon after a male friend had left her house. The man told police he had heard strange noises outside Janelle's bedroom window before he left, but she said they came from the washing machine.

Reeled in

Then the killer vanished completely. In 1977 and 1978, he had begun to call his victims, threatening to kill one of them. He phoned the police, taunting them, and sent a poem to Sacramento's mayor's office, the local TV station and the *Sacramento Bee*. Another victim got a call in 2001 after the *Sacramento Bee* had published an article reporting that the Original Night Stalker had been linked to the East Area Rapist by DNA evidence, making him the Golden State Killer.

The trail had gone well and truly cold in 2016 when the FBI uploaded the DNA profile to a genetic heritage website and found ten to 20 people who had the same great-great-great-grandparents as the Golden State Killer. From that, it was possible to construct a family tree. That narrowed the field down to two suspects. DeAngelo was finally identified when samples of his DNA were covertly collected from the door handle of his car and a tissue in his garbage can. Arrested, he pleaded guilty to 13 counts of first-degree murder and 13 counts of kidnapping. He was sentenced to life without possibility of parole.

ISRAEL KEYES: TED BUNDY WANNABE

A n admirer of Ted Bundy, the prolific serial killer in the 1970s who was executed in 1989, Israel Keyes did everything he could to emulate his idol – targeting total strangers, avoiding anyone he had any possible connection to, travelling hundreds of miles to target random victims in secluded parks and other remote locations. But he was eventually caught because he broke all his own rules.

After confessing to as many as 12 murders, Israel Keyes was asked why he did it. He replied: 'Why not?' His motivation was pleasure, said Monique Doll, an Anchorage homicide detective who worked on the case.

'Israel Keyes didn't kidnap and kill people because he was crazy,' she told a news conference. 'He didn't kidnap and kill people because his deity told him to or because he had a bad childhood. Israel Keyes did this because he got an immense amount of enjoyment out of it, much like an addict gets an immense amount of enjoyment out of drugs.'

ISRAEL KEYES

FBI Special Agent Jolene Goeden said: 'He liked what he was doing. He talked about the rush he got out of it, the adrenaline and kind of the high from it. In a way, he was an addict, and he was addicted to the feeling that he got when he was doing this.'

However, Keyes was very different from his hero. Bundy went after a very specific victim, typically a young white woman who had long, straight hair parted down the middle. Keyes had no victim type. He would go after both men and women. He didn't care about ethnicity. Most serial killers, when they first start to kill, go after a victim they think won't be missed – people from vulnerable populations like sex workers and runaways. But Keyes would take people alone and in pairs. And he would take them in broad daylight from very public places.

He liked to go people-hunting in the daylight in national parks, campgrounds, lakes and beaches. He told investigators he would also hunt for victims in cemeteries because nobody ever questions a person on their own in a cemetery. But then he would also take people in the dead of night from their own bedrooms in well-off suburbs where such heinous crimes would normally be unthinkable.

Racist theology

Born in Richmond, Utah in 1978, Israel Keyes was the second of ten siblings. The family was religious and patriotic. His elder sister was called America. After leaving the Mormon faith, the Keyes family settled in Colville, Washington, where they attended several different branches of the Christian Identity church. Some followers of Christian Identity theology believe white people of Western European origin are the true descendants of Biblical Israelites. They promote racist beliefs and predict an apocalyptic race war that will be engineered by the Jews.

All of the Keyes children were delivered as home births and they never saw a doctor. They were home taught and none of them ever

176

went to school. For their first seven years in Washington state, they lived in a tent on a mountainside, while their father built them a cabin by hand. It did not have electricity or running water. As the oldest boy, Israel was taught how to kill and dress game to feed the family, while the father was either working down the mountain or out in the woods praying for hours on end.

Israel was reportedly friends with Chevie and Cheyne Kehoe, noted white supremacists who committed a number of high-profile crimes. In 1998, the Kehoe brothers got into a shootout with Ohio State Troopers. Chevie was later sentenced to life in prison for the murders of a gun dealer, his wife and her child. In 2014, Cheyne and father Kirby Kehoe would join him in prison on weapons charges.

Eventually, Keyes would reject his family's religious inclinations, along with the teachings of the Christian Identity church. When he told his parents that he was an atheist, they kicked him out and his siblings were told never to talk to him again.

Later, he would have a child with a Native American woman and live on the Makah Reservation where he worked for the tribal authority. Nevertheless, he admitted to harbouring a lifelong fantasy of killing a police officer, which he attributed to his white supremacist roots.

Murderous desires

From an early age, he had all the makings of a serial killer. By the age of ten, he was breaking and entering, stealing guns and setting fires. By 14, he was torturing and killing household pets. At 16, he raped a teenager. He managed to lure the girl away from her friends. He said he'd intended to kill her, but in the end he let her go.

It is thought he committed his first murders as a teenager near his home in Colville. Two teenage girls were killed in two separate incidents, along with one of the girls' mothers. But nothing was proved.

He joined the military at 20, though he did not have a birth certificate or a social security number. He served in the US Army from 1998 until 2000, but quit so that he could travel freely and commit murder. During his time in the army, he said he did not kill, but admitted to two rapes – one while he was stationed in Egypt and another on leave in Israel.

After leaving the service, he worked as a handyman, paying for his travel with burglary and by robbing banks. In 2007, he moved to Anchorage, Alaska with his girlfriend and their daughter. There he set up a construction business. But the desire to murder was too much for him.

He kept what he called 'murder kits' near his home in Anchorage and in New York state where he had a rundown cabin on ten acres of land. The one found in Alaska included a shovel, plastic bags and bottles of Drano, which he told authorities would speed up the decomposition of bodies. The murder kit found in upstate New York contained weapon parts, a silencer, ligatures, ammunition and garbage bags. Keyes said other murder kits were hidden in Washington state, Wyoming, Texas and somewhere in the southwest, possibly Arizona. There was also one in Vermont, which he had hidden there two years before he committed a double murder near to its hiding place.

Despite this meticulous planning, he wanted to kill so much that the urge sometimes got the better of him. In the spring of 2011, he targeted two people in an Anchorage park to try out a silencer he had put on a rifle that he would later use in Vermont. However, a police officer arrived and told the intended victims the park was closed. Keyes later told investigators that he almost pulled the trigger on all three, but then another officer arrived.

'That could have got ugly,' Keyes said in a recorded interview. 'Fortunately for the cop guy, his backup showed up.'

Evil outlook

Generally, he said, he did not like shooting people. He preferred strangling them, so that he could savour their life slowly ebbing away.

On the spur of the moment, on 1 February 2012, he kidnapped 18-year-old barista, Samantha Koenig, in Anchorage. CCTV footage showed him approaching her kiosk as she was closing up at around 8pm and ordering an Americano. While she was making it, he pulled a gun. He climbed into the kiosk and bound her hands behind her back with zip ties, before leading her out. She had not pushed the panic button because he told her that he would let her go if her parents paid a ransom. This was never his intention.

Her family reported her missing the following morning, but the police did nothing. She had only been working there for a couple of weeks. They thought that she was a teenage girl who probably came from a rough background, a broken home and had a history with drugs. She had most likely made off with the day's taking from the register – a couple of hundred bucks maybe – and she was out partying. She'd come back when she felt like it.

This was not the case at all. The truth was far more brutal. The FBI reckoned that Koenig had put up a fight. She had broken away at some point and Keyes chased her, tackling her to bring her to the ground. Pointing his gun at her, he said she should not do anything to make him kill her.

More video footage showed him forcing her into the back of his 2004 Chevrolet Silverado in the parking lot of Home Depot. The police drew up a list of 750 white trucks of the same make in the area, but the licence plate, toolboxes and a ladder rack he usually carried had been removed before the abduction. They were reinstalled afterwards, effectively disguising the vehicle.

Samantha was sexually assaulted and strangled. Her body was left in a cold shed for two weeks, while her killer went on a cruise. When he returned, he posed her body and sewed her eyes open with fishing line to make it look like she was still alive. Then he photographed her alongside a newspaper dated 13 February, 12 days after the abduction. The FBI had to call in an expert to determine whether she was dead or alive.

Israel Keyes.

On the back of the photograph, he wrote a ransom note demanding $30,000 from her family. He then sent a text to her boyfriend from her cellphone, telling him where to find the note in a nearby park. Otherwise, the batteries were removed from the cellphone, so it could not be traced. While maintaining the fiction that he was holding her hostage for ransom, he dismembered her body and dropped it in a frozen lake north of Anchorage, after cutting a hole through the ice with a chainsaw.

The next mistake he made was using her debit card on a trip to the southwestern US. His rental car was caught on video when he used it at an ATM in Texas. When he was stopped for speeding, federal agents were already on his trail and he was arrested.

Hideous crimes

Extradited back to Alaska, he admitted a series of burglaries, bank robberies and murders, though he fell silent when his name was leaked to the press. The authorities had difficulty identifying the murder victims as Keyes rarely knew their names.

He was suspected of kidnapping mothers and children from a shopping mall in Boca Raton, Florida in three separate incidents. The first two times, he shot mother and child and left their bodies in their vehicles. The third time, he let them go unharmed after several hours. Though he was wearing a mask, the mother glimpsed his face and he answered to the same general description as Keyes. He might also have murdered a woman believed to be Debra Feldman in April 2009 in New Jersey, and buried her near Tupper Lake, New York.

He also admitted to a number of bank robberies in New York and Texas and was a suspect in the murder of Jimmy Tidwell, an electrician who disappeared near Longview, Texas on 15 February 2012. During a bank robbery the following day in Azle, Texas, about 170 miles from Longview, the culprit – believed to be Keyes – wore a white hard hat similar to Tidwell's. The FBI say he also burgled homes and committed arson.

The victims of the double murder he admitted to in Vermont were identified as William and Lorraine Currier, a middle-aged couple who lived in the village of Essex. He flew from Anchorage to Chicago and then drove a thousand miles to their home. He chose it because it had an attached garage where he could hide his car. There was no evidence of children or a dog, and he was familiar with that style of house and knew where the master bedroom was.

He broke into their bedroom, bound the couple with zip ties, forced them into their vehicle and drove them to an abandoned farmhouse. There, he shot William and sexually assaulted and strangled Lorraine. The house has since been torn down, but their bodies were never found. However, Samantha Koenig's body parts were recovered from the lake in Alaska.

Having spent much of his life living under the radar, Keyes became one of those rare creatures – a serial killer who was never convicted of murder. But he still paid the ultimate price. He slashed his wrists and strangled himself with a bed sheet in jail while awaiting trial. With no one to try, the case had to be dropped.

MELVIN REES:
THE SEX BEAST

On 26 June 1957, Margaret Harold was driving in rural Maryland with her boyfriend, an unnamed US Army sergeant, when they were forced off the road by a green Chrysler. The driver walked over to them and indicated that they should wind down the window. He was carrying a gun. It seems he climbed into the back seat and asked for cigarettes and money. When they refused, he shot Margaret Harold in the face.

Realizing that his life was in danger, the sergeant fled. Finding refuge in an isolated farmhouse a mile away, he called the police. When they arrived, they found that Margaret had been stripped naked and her dead body had been sexually abused. The killer was quickly dubbed 'The Sex Beast'.

The sergeant gave a good description of the slim, dark-haired assailant. It was little to go on. Searching the area for anything the killer might have dropped, the police found a deserted cinder-block building with a broken basement window. Inside, they found violent pornography and pictures of a dead woman undergoing a post-mortem taped to the walls. This appeared to be the killer's lair.

Among the pictures, one stood out. It came out of a class yearbook from the University of Maryland. It showed Wanda Tipton, who had graduated in 1955. As this was their only clue, detectives tracked her down, but she insisted she knew no one who matched the description given by the sergeant. The trail went cold – until the same killer struck again.

On 11 January 1959, Carroll and Mildred Jackson, and their two daughters, 18-month-old Janet and five-year-old Susan, went missing. Driving home from a family reunion in Apple Grove, West Virginia to Falls Church, Virginia, a relative spotted their car abandoned at the side of the road. The car was empty and, when they were called, the police could find no sign of a struggle. The Jacksons, it seemed, had vanished.

Soon after the Jacksons' disappearance, a local couple came forward to report that the same afternoon a blue Chevrolet had driven up behind them, flashing its headlights and forcing them off the road. A dark-haired man with a menacing manner got out of his car and approached the couple. Sensing danger, they reversed and fled. The man's description matched the one that the army sergeant had given.

Two months later, Carroll Jackson's body was found in a ditch. His hands were tied behind his back and he had been shot in the back of the head. Under him was baby Janet who had been dumped in the ditch alive and suffocated under the weight of her father's body. Two weeks after that, two boys out squirrel hunting found a shallow grave. In it were the bodies of Susan and Mildred. Both had been raped and bludgeoned to death. Mildred had also been tortured and forced to perform oral sex on her assailant. In a building nearby – seemingly the same cinder-block building as before – the police found a red button from Mildred's dress. Outside, there were tyre marks from a Chevrolet.

High on Benzedrine

The police then received an anonymous letter naming 26-year-old jazz musician Melvin Rees as a possible suspect. It had come from Glen Moser, who said he had a conversation with Rees the night before the Jacksons disappeared.

High on Benzedrine, Rees had outlined his views on the then fashionable existential philosophy, asserting: 'You can't say it's wrong to kill. Only individual standards make it right or wrong.'

He also named Rees as a suspect in the Margaret Harold case. They had been working together in the area at the time. The police tried to track down Rees, but he had moved, leaving no forwarding address. But they discovered that he had been to the University of Maryland, so they contacted Wanda Tipton again. She admitted that Rees had been her boyfriend, but she had broken it off after he told her he was already married.

A talented player of the saxophone, clarinet and piano, Rees had dropped out of college before graduating and made a living playing in jazz clubs around Washington, DC. In 1955, he had been arrested for assaulting an unidentified 36-year-old woman. She said he had tried to force her into his car, but she had escaped. However, the woman decided not to press charges and the case was dropped.

It was found that Rees had moved in with stripper and would-be actress Pat Barrington. They had been living in Hyattsville, Maryland but had since moved on.

Unable to find Rees, the police called in Dutch psychic Peter Hurkos, who would later be involved in the hunt for the Boston Strangler and the investigation of the Manson Family. After visiting the scenes of the crimes and the victims' graves, and handling some of their possessions, he named a different suspect, but the man he picked out lived at Rees's former address. Nevertheless, his contribution was ridiculed by the *Washington Post*.

Melvin Rees.

As the investigation was going nowhere, Moser abandoned his anonymity. He went to the police with a letter he had received from his old friend Rees, who was then working in a piano store in West Memphis where the FBI arrested him.

At his home, they found a .38 calibre handgun in a saxophone case. It was the gun that had been used to kill Margaret Harold and Carroll Jackson. Along with it was a newspaper cutting carrying a picture of Mildred Jackson and a note, saying: 'Drove to select area and killed husband and baby. Now the mother and daughter are all mine.' It went on to describe the sadistic torture of Mildred, concluding: 'Then tied and gagged, led her to a place of execution and hung [sic] her. I was her master.'

Tried in Maryland, Rees was found guilty of the murder of Margaret Harold and sentenced to life imprisonment. Then in Virginia, he was convicted of the murders of the Jackson family and sentenced to death, but capital punishment had been suspended in the US before the death sentence was carried out. He died in prison in 1995.

Rees was linked to four more homicides around the University of Maryland. All of the victims were teenagers and had been raped. Their names were Mary Shomette, Michael Ann ('Mikie') Ryan, Mary Fellers, and Shelby Venable. In 1985, while in prison, Rees talked with a reporter and confessed to the murders of Shelby Venable and Mary Fellers. He was never charged with either crime.

PAUL DUROUSSEAU:
THE KILLER CABBIE

At around 10.30pm on 1 January 2003, relatives of 19-year-old Nikia Shanell Kilpatrick visited her apartment in the Spanish Oaks neighbourhood of Jacksonville, Florida. They were worried because no one in the family had heard from her over the holiday period. When they arrived at the apartment block, they saw Nikia's two-year-old son banging on the window. Inside the apartment, there was a putrid smell and her younger son, who was just 11 months old, was crawling about on the floor.

Nikia's decomposing body was found in the bedroom. She had been tied up and there was a cord around her neck. She had been strangled and sexually abused. The medical examiner found that she had been killed up to 48 hours before her body had been discovered. The children had survived by eating dried food from the kitchen. They were malnourished and traumatized by being confined with their dead mother. Worse, Nikia had been six months pregnant at the time of her death.

While the police found some vital physical evidence at the crime scene, nothing immediately pointed to a suspect. However, there were some clues. The perpetrator clearly was organized. It was surmised that this was not his first murder. Indeed, less than two weeks before, on 19 December 2002, the remains of 18-year-old Nicole L. Williams had been found in a ditch. They were wrapped in a light-blue blanket from a Jacksonville hotel, where it was thought she had been murdered. Like Nikia, she had been bound and strangled.

On 10 January, 20-year-old nursing assistant, Shawanda Denise McCalister, was found dead in her Jacksonville apartment. Again, she had been bound and sexually abused, and she had a cord around her neck. She was also pregnant at the time of her death. Investigators drew the obvious parallel that her death was linked to those of Nikia Kilpatrick and Nicole Williams. DNA taken from the bodies showed that the same killer was responsible. Plainly, a serial killer was at work and he would soon be known as the Jacksonville Strangler.

The killer did not stop there. On 5 February, construction workers found the body of 17-year-old Jovanna Tyrica Jefferson in a ditch on a vacant lot. She had been missing since 20 January 2003. When the police arrived, they also found the remains of 19-year-old mother of two, Surita Ann Cohen, just six feet from Jovanna's. She had been missing since 4 February. Again, they had been tied up and sexually abused before they were strangled. An identical slipknot was used in each case. And, at last, there was a vital clue to the identity of the killer. Both women had been seen with a cab driver named Paul Durousseau before they disappeared.

Police record

Born on 11 August 1970 in Beaumont, Texas, Durousseau had a police record dating back to December 1991 when he was arrested in California for carrying a concealed handgun. He had been living with his mother's family in Los Angeles since his parents split. After graduating from high school, 19-year-old Durousseau found himself working as a security guard.

After a second offence in January 1992, he joined the US Army and was posted to Germany, where the authorities subsequently suspect he killed several women. While stationed there, he met and fell in love with a 21-year-old service woman named Natoca, who he had met in a nightclub. They married in Las Vegas, Nevada in 1995.

Stationed at Fort Benning, Georgia two years later, Durousseau was arrested and charged with kidnap and rape, but was acquitted on all charges. A month later, the naked body of a 26-year-old woman named Tracy Habersham was found in a ditch. She had been raped and strangled with a cord. At that time, Durousseau was not a suspect. Later, though, DNA would tie him to the case and he confessed.

Durousseau was then found in possession of stolen goods. Court-martialled in January 1999, he was dishonourably discharged from the army. Although this put a strain on his marriage, Durousseau and his wife moved to Jacksonville, her home town, where they raised two daughters. But he had a problem holding down a job and was described by acquaintances as a 'lewd womanizer'. It was said that he often made sexually suggestive comments to local women and tried to seduce young girls in the neighbourhood.

This did not go down well with acquaintances. Natoca was well liked, while Durousseau was seen as something of a wastrel. As well as bringing up the children, she worked and went to school. In August 1999, she went to the police after he slapped her and grabbed her around the neck in an argument about finances. They told her how to get a restraining order. She did not take their advice until the following year when he became angry and violent after she told him she was planning to file for divorce.

'I am afraid it will escalate,' she wrote in the petition. However, the restraining order was not issued after Natoca dropped the matter, though she sought another injunction 12 months later after he had put his hands around her neck and threatened to kill her.

Feeble sentence

In August 2001, he was jailed for six weeks for physically abusing his wife, after serving a month with two years' probation for the rape of a Jacksonville woman – an extraordinarily light sentence. Meanwhile, he had been arrested for trespassing on private property and in April 2001 he was charged with burglary, but later acquitted.

Despite a lengthening criminal record, he found temporary work – as a school bus driver and an animal control worker, aka a dog catcher. In January 2003, he began driving for Gator City Taxi, a Jacksonville cab company. This brought him into the company of many women, including Jovanna Jefferson and Surita Cohen.

Seventeen-year-old Jovanna Jefferson was last seen getting into a taxi driven by a man known as 'D'. When she did not return home, her aunt called her cellphone. It was answered by a man who identified himself as the cab driver who said she would be home soon. When she did not return, Jovanna's mother went to Gator City Taxi where she was told that 'D' was Paul Durousseau.

By then, Durousseau and his wife had split after eight and a half years of marriage. In January 2003, Natoca had moved into a new house with her daughters. While Durousseau continued living in the family home, he visited often. He was there when he was arrested for a violation of his probation for the 2001 rape case. While he was in Duval County Jail, the police built a case against him, matching his DNA to samples found on the victims. Other forensic evidence linked him to the crime scenes. They also had cellphone data and the cab company's records. It was then that Durousseau became known as the Killer Cabbie.

The evidence was overwhelming. As well as the DNA, jewellery belonging to Jovanna and Surita was found in his car. Cellphone records showed that the two girls had called him before they disappeared. Fibres from the blanket Nicole Williams was wrapped in were found in his home. And a surveillance tape from an ATM Shawanda McCalister had withdrawn money from on the day she died showed Durousseau in the background.

On 17 June 2003, Paul Durousseau was charged with five counts of first-degree murder for the deaths of Nikia Kilpatrick, Shawanda McCalister, Nicole Williams, Jovanna Jefferson and Surita Cohen. He also faced two counts of child abuse against Nikia's son who he left alone in the apartment for two days with the decomposing remains of their mother.

Charges for the murder of Tracy Habersham followed. She was last seen alive in September 1997 at a party in the NCO Club at Fort Benning, while he was stationed there. Her naked body was found a couple of days later in a ditch in nearby Columbus, Georgia. She had been strangled. Again, matching DNA linked him to the murder.

More followed. On 26 August 2003, he was charged with the 1999 murder of 24-year-old mother-of-three Tyresa Mack. She had been strangled in her Eastside apartment in Jacksonville. DNA samples matched and he had been seen leaving her apartment carrying a television.

A Florida grand jury indicted him on five counts of first-degree murder and two counts of child abuse for leaving Nikia Kilpatrick's children alone with their dead mother's body. The indictment was necessary for the state attorney to seek the death penalty. However, he did not pursue the deaths of the foetuses some of the victims were carrying that died along with their mothers. In the end, Durousseau only went on trial for the murder of Tyresa Mack. The other murder charges were dropped, though they could be reinstated if he was not executed. Meanwhile, the parents of three of the victims sued Gator City Taxi for failing in their duty to carry out adequate background checks on Durousseau before hiring him.

At the trial, Durousseau spent about 90 minutes on the stand, answering questions about his relationships with the dead women. He admitted having sex with Tyresa Mack, Nikia Kilpatrick and Shawanda McCalister before their deaths, but insisted he wasn't the one who killed them. He admitted lying to detectives when he initially denied knowing any of them.

He said he met Mack in April 1999 and that they had met often for three months. The last time he saw her was on 26 July, the day she was killed, and she was alive when he left her apartment. When he heard about her death – he thought she'd been shot – he did not contact police as he didn't have any fresh information to give them.

On 13 December 2007, Paul Durousseau was convicted of first-degree murder and sentenced to death by lethal injection. Mack's sister, Latashia Bell, said: 'He's getting what he deserves. I know it won't bring my sister back, but I do have closure – me and my family.'

But before the sentence could be carried out, state law had been changed to require a unanimous verdict, including in some cases retroactively, for the death penalty to be carried out. In Durousseau's trial, the jury had only found for the death penalty by a majority of ten to two. The high court rejected arguments for a new trial. However, a new jury was constituted for a fresh sentencing hearing. Again, it returned a majority of ten to two. On 10 December 2021, after over ten years on death row, Durousseau was sentenced to life imprisonment without possibility of parole.

WAYNE BERTRAM WILLIAMS: THE ATLANTA CHILD KILLER

Racism is endemic in the United States, especially in the southern, formerly slave-owning states, so when, in the summer of 1979, a two-year spate of slaying black children and young people began in Atlanta, Georgia, it was natural to assume that the killer was white. Suspicion fell on Charles T. Sanders, a white supremacist affiliated with the Ku Klux Klan, after he was secretly recorded praising the killer for 'wiping out a thousand future generations of n***ers'.

An informant told the Georgia Bureau of Investigation that Sanders said the KKK was 'creating an uprising among the blacks, that they were killing the children, that they are going to do one each month until things blow up'. The informant also told the police that Sanders had threatened to strangle one of the child victims, 14-year-old Lubie Geter, because Geter ran into Sanders' car in a go-cart. Geter was later strangled. However, the police dropped that line of investigation after seven weeks when Sanders and two of his brothers passed a lie-detector test.

Instead, blame has been pinned on African-American Wayne Bertram Williams, though in the end he was only convicted of the murder of two adults. He was never charged with the child slayings and has consistently denied the accusations throughout the 40 years he has been in jail. However, when working on the case, the originator of criminal profiling, former FBI agent John E. Douglas, concluded that the killer was black, so when Williams was arrested, he fitted the profile. In his 1995 book *Mindhunter* Douglas maintained that, in his opinion, 'forensic and behavioural evidence points conclusively to Wayne Williams as the killer of 11 young men in Atlanta', though not all 23 of the children who died or disappeared between 1979 and 1981 in Georgia's capital. Despite the fact that many have their doubts, in the mind of the authorities Wayne Williams is the Atlanta Child Killer.

Cluster of murders

The story began in the early hours of 21 July 1979, when 14-year-old Edward Hope Smith left the skating rink where he had spent the evening with his girlfriend to go home to one of Atlanta's dilapidated housing projects. Four days later, 14-year-old Alfred Evans left home on the other side of town to go and see a karate movie. Both of them were found dead on 28 July in a wooded area in the southwest of the city. Smith had been shot with a .22-calibre gun, while the medical examiner determined that Evans had died from asphyxia, possibly by strangulation. On the strength of a phone call, the police dismissed the killings as 'drug related'. That was the end of the matter.

On 4 September 1979, 14-year-old Milton Harvey, who had been taken out of the projects when his parents moved to a middle-class neighbourhood, borrowed a bicycle to take a cheque to the bank for his mother. The bike was found a week later abandoned on a deserted dirt track, while his body turned up in November, miles away on a rubbish dump just outside the city limits. At first, his death was not considered a homicide and no signs of violence could be discerned on his badly decomposed body.

A few weeks before Harvey's body had been found, nine-year-old Yusef Bell disappeared on his way to the store to buy snuff for a neighbour. Police dismissed the testimony of a witness who said she had seen Yusef getting into a blue car with a man she believed to be the ex-husband of Yusef's mother. The boy's body was found on 8 November stuffed into a hole in the floor of an abandoned elementary school. He had been strangled. Mayor Maynard Jackson, Atlanta's first black mayor, promised a full investigation, though, as yet, the four deaths had not been connected.

The killings continue

On 10 March 1980 12-year-old Angel Lenair was found tied to a tree. She had been strangled with an electrical cord and a pair of panties – not her own – were shoved down her throat. There was evidence of sexual abuse, though the medical examiner did not find this conclusive.

The following day, ten-year-old Jeffery Mathis did not return from an errand he was running for his mother. Again, he had been seen getting into a blue car. The witness said that, when he saw the driver later, he had pulled a gun on him. Mathis's brothers said that they had seen a blue car in the driveway of a house that Jeffery was known to visit. Boys from his school had complained that two black men in a blue car had attempted to lure them away from the schoolyard. They had memorized the licence plate and reported it to police, but the authorities did little to investigate.

Then on 18 May, 14-year-old Eric Middlebrooks got a phone call at about 10pm. He grabbed his tools and told his foster mother that he was going out to fix his bike. His body was found a few blocks away the following morning. He had been bludgeoned to death. His bike was nearby. The police assumed he had been the unwitting witness to a robbery. That, again, was the end of the matter.

The pace quickened with what became known as the 'Summer of Death'. On 22 June, seven-year-old LaTonya Wilson was abducted from her home. An African-American man was seen climbing through her bedroom window. He was seen exiting the back door, then stopping to chat to another black man with a lifeless LaTonya under his arm. The body of LaTonya Wilson was found in mid-October, not far from her home. It was too badly decomposed to determine the cause of death.

The following day, ten-year-old Aaron Wyche went missing. His body was found under a bridge on a six-lane highway. He had died from asphyxia, though the medical examiner said this was because of the way he had landed when he fell from the parapet. But Aaron was afraid of heights and was unlikely to have climbed on to the bridge voluntarily. He had also been seen getting into a blue car.

Then on 6 July, nine-year-old Anthony Carter disappeared while playing hide and seek. His body was found behind a warehouse less than a mile from home. He had been stabbed to death. On 30 July, 11-year-old Earl Terrell disappeared after leaving a swimming pool. A man called his aunt and told her that he had taken Earl to Alabama and it would cost her $200 to get him back. He did not call again. The police suspected a child pornography ring had been operating across the street from the pool. John David Wilcoxen was arrested after thousands of indecent photographs were found. A witness said that Earl Terrell had visited Wilcoxen's house several times, but the police dismissed any connection to the missing black children because the kids in Wilcoxen's pictures were all white.

It was clear that, for whatever reason, the police were doing a pretty bad job. But the disappearance of Earl Terrell gave Mayor Jackson the excuse he needed. If he had been taken across the state line into Alabama, his abduction was a federal matter and he called in the FBI. They soon had more to investigate.

Growing list of victims

On 20 August, the body of 13-year-old Clifford Jones, who had come to Atlanta to visit his grandmother, was found in a dumpster. He had been strangled and the shorts and underwear he was wearing were not his. Evidence suggested that the manager of a local laundromat was responsible. He admitted knowing Clifford, who had been at the laundromat that evening. A young witness said that he had seen him beat and strangle a black boy, and dump him with the trash. Nothing was done as the police dismissed the informant as 'retarded'.

Twelve-year-old Charles Stephens went missing on 9 October 1980. His body was found on a hillside the following morning. He had died from suffocation. A drug dealer said that he had seen the boy, dead, on the back seat of a client's car. The client threatened him with a gun, saying he would kill him if he said anything. The dealer said the man was a known paedophile.

A task force was set up. Soon the list of potential victims swelled to 60, though many similar cases were left off. Twenty-two-year-old Faye Yearby was found tied to a tree like Angel Lenair in January 1981. She had been stabbed to death, but she was left off the list as she was thought to be too old. Ten-year-old Darron Glass, who disappeared on 14 September 1980, was also left off because he had run away several times before. Nevertheless, city patrols were stepped up and a curfew was imposed for Halloween in case the killer targeted trick-or-treaters.

Investigator Chet Dettlinger, author of *The List*, spotted that the places where the victims were last seen, or their bodies dumped, were confined to specific areas along certain highways and that a number of the victims knew each other. Nine-year-old Aaron Jackson was a friend of Aaron Wyche. His body was found under a bridge in November 1980. He had been smothered in the same manner as Charles Stephens.

Aaron Jackson was also friends with 16-year-old Patrick 'Pat Man' Rogers, a karate fan and singer who had a crush on Aaron's sister. With connections to at least 17 other victims, Rogers disappeared on 10 November. Like Darron Glass, he was thought to have run away. Before he left, Rogers had told his mother that he had found someone to manage his singing career. The man's name was Wayne Williams. Rogers's body was found on 21 December 1980, face down in the Chattahoochee River. He had died from a blow to his head that had crushed his skull.

Then 14-year-old Lubie Geter disappeared on 3 January 1981 and was found the following month. He was wearing only his underwear. His body was badly decomposed and it was thought he had been strangled. He had connections to the suspect in the Terrell case and another possible paedophile.

Geter's friend, 15-year-old Terry Pue, disappeared soon after. An anonymous caller told the police where they could find his body. He had been strangled. The caller also said there was another body nearby. The remains were not found until years later and they were too badly decomposed to be identified, but they were thought to be those of Darron Glass.

Eleven-year-old Patrick Baltazar disappeared on 6 February 1981. Shortly before, the task force received a phone call from him, saying the killer was coming after him. They failed to respond. His body was found by a park attendant. He had been strangled and the rope thought to have been the murder weapon was discovered nearby. His teacher said she had received a phone call from a boy she thought to be Baltazar. The boy never said who he was; he merely cried into the phone.

On 6 March 1981, the body of 13-year-old Curtis Walker was found. He had been strangled. His uncle, who he lived with in the projects, had also been murdered but was not included on the list. The same day, the remains of ten-year-old Jeffery Mathis were found. He had been missing for almost a year and his funeral made the national news.

Fifteen-year-old Joseph 'Jo-Jo' Bell went missing on 2 March 1981. Two days later, a co-worker at Cap'n Peg's seafood restaurant said that Bell called him, saying he was 'almost dead' and begged for his help before hanging up the phone. The manager called the police. Bell's mother then received a call from a woman, saying she had Jo-Jo. Mrs Bell contacted the task force who, again, did not respond. His body was found on 19 April 1981 in the South River. Cause of death: probable asphyxia.

Eleven days after Jo-Jo went missing, his friend Timothy Hill also disappeared. Together, they had visited the home of paedophile Thomas Terrell – no relation to Earl – who, it was said, paid Hill for sex. The body of 13-year-old Timothy Hill was found in the Chattahoochee River on 30 March 1981. Cause of death: asphyxia. Hill had connections to Alfred Evans, Jeffrey Mathis, Patrick Baltazar and Anthony Carter.

City of fear

By then, rivers had become the killer's preferred dumping ground and the victims were becoming progressively older. The city was on the alert and vigilante groups roamed the projects.

On 20 March 1981, 21-year-old Eddie 'Bubba' Duncan, a boy with physical and learning difficulties, went missing. He had connections to Patrick Rogers. On 8 April 1981, his body was found in the Chattahoochee River. Cause of death: probable asphyxia. He made the list, though earlier he would have been considered too old.

Twenty-year-old Larry Rogers – no relation to Patrick Rogers – made the list in April 1981 when his body was found in an abandoned apartment. He also had learning difficulties and had been strangled. He, too, had connections to Wayne Williams who had protected Larry's younger brother after he had got into a fight, giving him refuge in an apartment near where Larry was found dead.

Twenty-three-year-old ex-convict, Michael McIntosh, lived across the street from Cap'n Peg's seafood restaurant where Jo-Jo Bell had worked. He disappeared on 25 March 1981 after telling a store owner that he had been beaten up by two black men. He, too, had been seen at Thomas Terrell's house, or Uncle Tom's as it was known. His body was found in the Chattahoochee River in April. Cause of death: probable asphyxia.

Ex-convict John Porter was 28 when he went missing. He had mental problems and had been caught fondling a two-year-old boy. His body was found on the sidewalk of an empty lot in April 1981. He had been stabbed six times and dumped in the empty lot. At first, he did not make the list. This changed when he was linked to Wayne Williams by forensic evidence presented at the trial.

Twenty-one-year-old ex-con Jimmy Ray Payne had disappeared the same month. He had been depressed while in jail for burglary and had tried to hang himself. His body was found floating in the Chattahoochee River. It had been in the water for a week and the cause of death could not be determined.

William Barrett, aka Billy Star, a 17-year-old juvenile delinquent, went missing in May on his way to pay a bill for his mother. His body was found close to home. He had been strangled and stabbed, and he had connections to Lubie Geter and a convicted paedophile they both knew.

Stakeout

In the early hours of 22 May 1981, the police were staking out the James Jackson Parkway Bridge across the Chattahoochee River when they heard a loud splash. They stopped a white 1970 Chevrolet station wagon on the bridge above. The driver was Wayne Williams.

Asked what he was doing, Williams, a small-time music promoter, said he was on his way to audition a singer named Cheryl Johnson. But neither the address nor the phone number he gave for her checked out. Two days later, the naked body of 27-year-old ex-con Nathaniel Carter was fished out of the Chattahoochee River, downstream. Cause of death: probably asphyxia. Carter was an acquaintance of Michael McIntosh and lived in the same apartment block as LaTonya Wilson. He was a gay prostitute, drug dealer and an alcoholic. Due to his irregular lifestyle, it is not known when he disappeared.

Williams was charged with the murder of Nathaniel Carter and Jimmy Payne. Until the last moment, the prosecution withheld the information that four witness had said they had seen Carter alive after 22 May. They were not called. The prosecution case relied on forensic evidence supplied by the FBI. This, they alleged, tied Williams to ten of the murders – mention of the other cases was allowed in court to show a pattern in the killings. Fibre from the bodies matched fabrics found in Williams's home and his car. Although these fabrics were ubiquitous, the defence did not have the money to contest the forensic evidence given by the FBI labs.

Witnesses testified that Williams had been seen with a number of the victims. He was shown to be a habitual liar and did himself no favours when he lost his temper while being cross-examined. He was convicted and given two life sentences. The Atlanta police then announced that 22 of the 29 cases on the list had been solved. But many people, including the Georgia state supreme court justices, former prosecutors and victims' family members, found the conviction of Williams unsafe.

It was said that if a white man had been found to be the Atlanta Child Killer, rioting – if not a full-blown race war – would have kicked off.

The investigation was re-opened in 2005. Doubt was cast over the forensic evidence and Charles T. Sanders was reported to have said that he was lucky that he wasn't arrested since he had the same type of carpet as Williams. Hair found on the bodies could not be shown definitively to have come from Williams. But the report said this: 'Wayne Williams cannot be excluded as the source of the hair.'

Hardly proof beyond reasonable doubt. Nevertheless, at time of writing, Williams remains in jail and will probably die there.

COLIN IRELAND:
THE GAY SLAYER

A t the age of 39, petty criminal Colin Ireland was directionless and wanted to do something with his life, so he decided to become a serial killer and read up on the subject. Known in the press as 'The Gay Slayer', he picked as his victims gay men who enjoyed the passive role in sadomasochistic sex as they would volunteer to be tied up before he murdered them.

Ireland claimed not to be gay himself. He had been married twice and had not engaged in sex with his victims, but he said he had pretended to be gay to pick them up. From his reading, he knew about 'geographic profiling' – the theory that a serial killer is likely to kill close to work or home. He lived in Southend-on-Sea in Essex, England, so he chose London as his killing ground. His stalking ground would be The Coleherne, a gay pub in the Earl's Court area. He would accompany the victims to their home and kill them there.

In a rucksack, he would carry a 'murder kit' – some cord, a knife, a pair of gloves, shoes and a change of clothes. After the murder, he would meticulously tidy up and clean the scene of the crime to ensure that he left no clues. To avoid suspicion, he would not leave the victim's flat late at night. Rather, he would wait until the morning when he would mingle with people going to work. Taking the train home, he would throw the clothes, shoes and gloves he had worn when he committed the murder out of the window, so they landed on some remote stretch of railway property where they were unlikely to be found.

On the other hand, he was not shy about publicity. On 9 March 1993, he called the newsroom of the *Sun* newspaper in London.

'I've murdered a man,' he told the journalist who answered. 'I'm calling you because I'm worried about his dogs. I want them to be let out. It would be cruel for them to be stuck there.'

It seems he was not at all concerned about his victim and gave an address in Battersea where the body, and the dogs, could be found.

'I tied him up and I killed him and I cleaned up the flat afterwards,' he said. 'I did it. It was my New Year resolution to kill a human being. Is that of any interest to you? He was a homosexual and into kinky sex.'

The newspaper alerted the police, who went to the address he had given. Forcing open the door, they found 45-year-old theatre director Peter Walker naked and spreadeagled on his four-poster bed with his wrists and ankles tied to each corner. There was a plastic bag over his head. As he could not have done this with his hands tied, someone else must have been with him. But was it murder or an erotic game gone badly wrong?

There were other odd clues, though. Two teddy bears had been left in a soixante-neuf position and a condom had been shoved in his mouth, another up a nostril. Ireland had done this because, while searching the flat, he said, he discovered that Walker was HIV-positive.

Mounting death toll

On 30 May 1993, the body of 37-year-old librarian Christopher Dunn was found tied, handcuffed and gagged at his home in Wealdstone, northwest London. He was naked except for a leather bondage harness and he had a plastic bag over his head. His testicles appeared to have been scorched. Later, it was discovered that £200 had been taken from his bank account. Ireland had tortured him to reveal the PIN number of his debit card. As Ireland was unemployed, he felt he needed money to pay for his train travel, new clothes and shoes, and other expenses.

Again, the police wondered whether his death was the result of a sex game and, as Wealdstone was on the other side of London from Battersea, they did not connect the case to that of Peter Walker. Ireland was free to kill again.

On 4 June, 35-year-old American executive, Perry Bradley III, was found at his home in Kensington, bound, gagged and strangled – £100 was missing from his wallet and £200 had been taken from his bank account. Apparently, Bradley was not into S&M, but Ireland had persuaded him to let him tie him up, saying that it was necessary for his arousal.

Three days later, 33-year-old housing warden Andrew Collier was found dead, tied to his bed in Dalston, northeast London. He had been strangled. Various parts of his body had been burnt, but he refused to give up his PIN. Frustrated, Ireland strangled his cat in front of him, before killing him. Ireland had to make do with £70 in cash he found in the flat. Again, during the search, he found that Collier was HIV-positive. He put a condom on Collier's penis and put it in the cat's mouth, then put a condom on the cat's tail and put that in Collier's mouth.

Feeling that he was not getting the publicity he deserved, Ireland taunted the police with a series of telephone calls. Before Collier's body was discovered, he told the police that he had read the *FBI Crime Classification Manual* before he decided to become a serial killer.

'I know what it takes to become one. You have to kill one over four to qualify, don't you? I have already killed three,' he said. According to the FBI, three qualifies. 'It started as an exercise, I wanted to see if it could be done, to see if I could really get away with it ... Have you found Christopher Dunn yet? I killed him too. I haven't seen anything in the papers.'

A few days later, the caller explained why he had killed Collier's cat. 'I don't want anybody to get any wrong ideas about me. I am not an animal lover,' he said.

Confessing to the murder of Perry Bradley, he said: 'I did the American. You've got some good leads on my identity from clues at the scene.'

In another anonymous call, Ireland said: 'Are you still interested in the death of Peter Walker? Why have you stopped the investigation? Doesn't the death of a homosexual man mean anything? I will do another. I have always dreamed of doing the perfect murder.'

Police inquiries soon established that at least three of the victims were regulars at The Coleherne, which was close to Bradley's flat. Then on the night of 12 June, 43-year-old Maltese-born chef Emmanuel Spiteri disappeared from The Coleherne. Three days later, police received another phone call.

'Have you found the body in southeast London yet, and the fire?' the caller said.

Forcing the door of Spiteri's apartment in Catford, the police found him naked and bound. He had been strangled. An attempt had been made to set fire to a pile of furniture, but the flames had died out before the whole building went up.

Smile, you're on CCTV

To get from The Coleherne to Catford, Spiteri would have taken the underground to Charing Cross, where he would have caught an overground train to Catford. Reviewing the British Rail security footage, the police spotted Spiteri on the CCTV tapes several times. With him was a tall, heavily built man.

His picture was circulated widely, but no one came forward to say they knew the man. But Ireland, of course, recognized him. On 21 July, he walked into a solicitor's office in Southend and said he needed legal

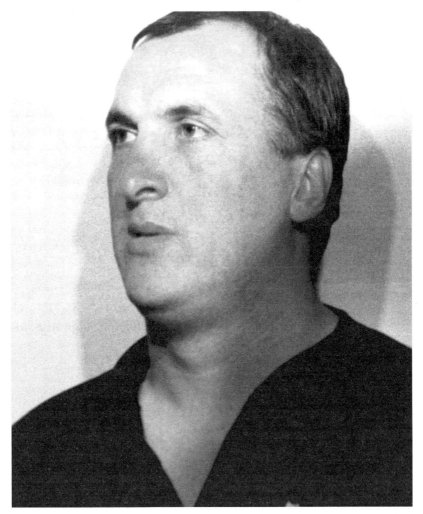

Colin Ireland.

representation. Ireland and the lawyer travelled up to London and went to the police together.

Ireland admitted he had been with Spiteri, but insisted he had left when another man arrived. But Ireland had made a fatal mistake. During his sojourn at Collier's home, there had been an altercation in the street outside. Looking out of the window, Ireland had touched the frame, leaving a fingerprint that he had overlooked when cleaning up. Confronting Ireland with this evidence, they expected a full confession. However, Ireland remained obstinately silent.

After two days of intensive questions, Ireland still admitted nothing and was remanded in prison.

'He will still be hearing the questions you ask him,' said criminal psychologist Paul Britton. 'He has to set the record straight. That's when he'll confess.'

After three weeks on remand, Ireland asked to speak to the police – 'but not those bastards who interviewed me. They really got under my skin.'

He then admitted all five murders, giving a detailed statement over the next two days. In it, he said he had not been under the influence of drugs or alcohol at the time of the murders. He was not gay or bisexual, even though he had once worked as a bouncer at a gay club in Soho. He had not undressed or engaged in any sexual activity with his victims and had gained no sexual thrill from the murders. And he held no grudge against the gay community. He had chosen gay men as his victims simply because they were easy targets.

But there was more to it. He claimed it was extreme male deviancy that triggered his anger as he had been approached by paedophiles as a child. He said his victims were deviants – being into S&M sex – who just happened to be gay. He claimed he was ridding society of vermin and considered himself a superior person.

Psychologists saw the strategic placing of items related to childhood on the victim's body – the teddy bears, the doll and the cat – as symbolic of Ireland's abhorrence at the loss of innocence. He himself was the victim of a disruptive childhood. He never knew his father and had been in and out of foster homes and borstals.

On 20 December 1993, at London's Old Bailey, Ireland was given five life sentences with a whole-life tariff. It was reported that he killed again in jail, strangling a convicted child killer in his cell, while in Wakefield prison, Yorkshire. As there was no possibility that he would ever be released there was no point in charging him. He died in prison in 2012, aged 57.

PETER TOBIN: BIBLE JOHN?

Serial killers usually begin their murderous careers in their twenties or thirties, so when 60-year-old Peter Tobin was found guilty of the rape and murder of 23-year-old Polish student Angelika Kluk on 4 May 2007, police forces across the UK began opening their cold-case files as Tobin already had a record of violent sexual offences.

In June, the police began searching 11 Robertson Avenue in Bathgate, West Lothian, where Tobin had lived in 1991. On 10 February that year, 15-year-old Vicky Hamilton disappeared after waiting for a bus less than a mile away. Tobin left Bathgate soon after.

Vicky's DNA was found, but though the house was stripped to a shell there was no sign of a body. Nevertheless, on 21 July 2007 Tobin was charged in connection with Vicky Hamilton's disappearance. The police went on to search 50 Irvine Drive in Margate, a property Tobin had occupied after he left Bathgate. They dug up the garden and found the body of Dinah McNicol, an 18-year-old sixth-former who lived in

Tillingham, Essex. She had been hitch-hiking home from a music festival in Hampshire when she disappeared.

Another body was found in the back garden at Irvine Drive. This proved to be that of Vicky Hamilton. The dismembered corpse was in plastic bin bags, which yielded Tobin's fingerprints. There were traces of semen. The DNA matched Tobin's.

Dinah's trousers and underwear had been pulled down over her buttocks, indicating a sexual assault had been attempted. Again, Tobin's fingerprints were found on the bin bags he had used to wrap the body and on the tape he used to seal them. Both bodies contained traces of amitriptyline, a date rape drug. Tobin was charged with the murders of the two young women.

Control freak

Born in Johnstone, Renfrewshire, on 27 August 1946, Tobin had a history of violent crime that stretched back over 40 years. He spent time in a young offender institution before serving jail terms for burglary, forgery and conspiracy. He also spent his adult life preying on vulnerable women. Outwardly, he was charming, affable and good-looking. His smart suits and flattery swept women off their feet. But his three former wives described him as a monster who sought to take total control of their lives, cutting them off from their friends and family while demeaning them in front of his.

His first wife, clerk-typist Margaret Mackintosh, was 17 when she married him in Brighton in 1969. Some 40 years later, she still bore the scars of a knife attack that he made on her. Tobin had stabbed her in the area of her vagina, leaving her bleeding heavily. The knife, he said, was a 'metal tampax'. If it had not been for the prompt action of a neighbour, she would have died.

'He raped me three or four times, enjoying my fear,' she said. 'When I put up a fight, I got a knife in my side. He left me to die on the bed.

Luckily, the man living underneath saw the blood coming through the ceiling and got me to hospital.'

When she tried to leave him, he decapitated the puppy that he had bought for her. After a year, she managed to escape and they divorced in 1971.

Tobin met his second wife, Sylvia Jefferies, in 1973. They had a son and a daughter who died soon after birth. Sylvia said that she lived in a constant state of fear.

'He'd whack me so hard it would send me flying across the room,' she said. In 1976, she left with their son.

His third wife was Cathy Wilson who, at 16, was more than 20 years his junior. They then moved to Bathgate in 1990, where he did odd jobs around the neighbourhood, usually fixing cars. They had a son, Daniel. But after two years of marriage, she found she had become a prisoner in her home. Tobin would not allow her to go outside.

'He was violent on almost a daily basis,' she said. 'He would push me against walls or put his hands round my neck for the simplest of things. If he said something and I dared to speak back or answer him in a way he thought disrespectful, he would blow up.'

Realizing that she had to escape, she waited until Tobin went out with a friend one night.

'He'd taken my car keys, house keys, money, bank books and my driving licence with him, but I had a stash of grocery money he didn't know about,' she said. 'It was only £25 but it paid for a bus ticket to Brighton.'

Soon after, Tobin was admitted to hospital after taking an overdose of the antidepressant amitriptyline, which was prescribed to relieve his anxiety. He told doctors that he had tried to commit suicide because his wife and child had left him 'without warning'. He later used the amitriptyline to subdue his victims.

On Friday 8 February 1991, Vicky Hamilton had left home in Redding near Falkirk to spend the weekend with her older sister in Livingston. Travelling back to Redding on Sunday evening, she had to change buses at Bathgate, where she vanished. The bus stop was just around the corner from Tobin's house.

False trail

Police scoured the neighbourhood, but they did not interview Tobin. He had only recently moved into the area and kept himself to himself.

Tobin then seized the opportunity to lay a false trail. Eleven days after Vicky had disappeared, Tobin went to Edinburgh, where he dropped Vicky's purse. It contained an identity card, her bus ticket, an address in London and a piece of paper with the word 'Samaritans' on it. A passer-by handed it in to the police. This distracted the investigation away from Bathgate, though later it would provide evidence against him. Traces of DNA belonging to his son were found on it.

Tobin then did a council-house swap with a couple in Margate. They spent days cleaning his house in Bathgate with bleach to try and get rid of the terrible smell. He arrived at 50 Irvine Drive with his secret cargo – the dismembered body of Vicky Hamilton – destined for a shallow grave in the back garden. Soon another corpse would join hers there.

On Saturday 3 August 1991, Dinah McNicol met David Tremett at the Torpedo Town Festival in Liphook, Hampshire. On Monday, they set off to hitch-hike back to their respective homes. They were picked up by a scruffy man in a green hatchback. Although David thought the man was a little odd, he chatted away to Dinah in the front seat.

When David got out at the turn-off for Redhill where he lived, he asked Dinah to come with him, but she was eager to get home to Tillingham. That was the last that was seen of her.

A neighbour saw Tobin digging the hole when he looked over the garden fence. Tobin told Martin that he was digging his way to Australia, joking that it was cheaper than paying the £10 fare on offer from the authorities at the time. Nine months later, the disappearance of Dinah McNicol featured on the TV show *Crimewatch*.

Despite their acrimonious divorce, Cathy Wilson still allowed Tobin to see their son Daniel. When the five-year-old went to stay with his father on 4 August 1993 in a flat he was renting in Havant, Hampshire, he walked into his dad's room to find two 14-year-old girls. One of them was unconscious. The two girls had called to visit the woman next door. When she was not in, Tobin invited them to wait in his place.

He gave them cider and vodka. One of them passed out; the other was sick. When she tried to wake her friend, Tobin threatened her with a knife and forced her to take a cocktail of pills and wine. Then she fought back and stabbed him in the leg. Hearing the commotion, Daniel came in, but Tobin ushered him out. Once the girl was unconscious, he raped and sodomized her.

Rat down a drainpipe

Afraid that the noise might have attracted others' attention, Tobin called Cathy at 2am, saying he was having a heart attack and telling her to come and collect Daniel. Once they were gone, Tobin turned on the gas and shinned down a drainpipe. But Britain had recently converted from coal gas, which was heavier than air and frequently used in suicide, to natural gas, which was lighter than air and easily dispersed.

One of the girls awoke to find her knickers round her ankles and her friend was lying next to her naked. She raised the alarm. The crime appeared on *Crimewatch*. Tobin was soon picked up. He pleaded guilty to the rape of one girl and the indecent assault of the other, and was sentenced to 14 years.

Released after ten years in 2004, Tobin returned to his native Scotland. In Paisley, he attacked 24-year-old Cheryl McLachlan with a kitchen knife. She called the police. Before they arrived, he had fled.

New persona

Adopting the name Pat McLaughlin, Tobin found refuge at St Patrick's Church in the Anderston area of Glasgow, which operated an open-door policy for the homeless. Employed as an odd-job man, he befriended Angelika Kluk. She was from the small town of Skoczów in Poland, but at the time lived just five minutes' walk from St Patrick's.

When she, too, found herself homeless, 62-year-old Father Nugent invited her to stay in the chapel house. Though Father Nugent was a Catholic priest, they became lovers. But Angelika soon took another lover, Martin MacAskill, a married man. When his wife found out, Martin took a holiday with her in Majorca in an attempt to patch things up.

Peter Tobin.

On 24 September 2006, just a few days before Angelika was due to return to Poland, she was helping Tobin paint a shed that they had built. She enjoyed his company since Father Nugent barely spoke to her and Martin was away.

Tobin had long wanted to have sex with her, so he clubbed her on the back on the head, bound and gagged her, then raped her. When Angelika fought back, Tobin grabbed a knife and stabbed her 19 times. He wrapped her body in a plastic sheet and shoved it down a hatch outside the confessional box, which was covered with a rug.

When Martin MacAskill returned to Scotland, he tried to contact Angelika. Unable to get her on her cellphone, he called her sister Aneta who was also living in Glasgow. Together, they searched Angelika's room. Nothing was missing, except her mobile. Martin called the police. Two constables arrived, searched the premises and took statements from everyone there, including the handyman.

The next day, Tobin left and took a bus to Edinburgh. Their suspicions aroused, the police searched the church again. They found a table-leg with Angelika's blood on it and several blood-soaked towels. In the bin, they found a pair of jeans with the left knee soaked in more of Angelika's blood. Eventually, the forensics team stumbled across the hatch in front of the confessional. In it, they found her body, still bound and gagged, along with a bloodstained kitchen knife.

Tobin checked himself into a hospital in Edinburgh under a false name, complaining of chest pains. The doctors could find nothing wrong with him and soon suspected that both the symptoms and the name were fictitious. The police arrived the next morning.

Tobin pleaded not guilty when he appeared in the High Court in Edinburgh the following March. After a six-week trial, Tobin was convicted of the murder of Angelika Kluk and sentenced to life, with a tariff of 21 years.

When Tobin went on trial for the murder of Vicky Hamilton in November 2008, the jury took less than two and a half hours to find him guilty. He was again sentenced to life with a minimum term of 30 years.

At his trial for the murder of Dinah McNicol in December 2009, the jury took just 13 minutes to deliver a unanimous verdict of guilty. The judge said he should never be released.

In jail, Tobin boasted to a prison psychiatrist that he had killed 48 women. There was speculation that Tobin was 'Bible John', the nickname given to the serial killer who murdered three women in Glasgow in the 1960s who has never been caught or identified. Detectives believed that there may have been other victims too – but Tobin would take these secrets to the grave. On 8 October 2022, aged 76, he died while serving three life sentences.

DÁMASO RODRÍGUEZ MARTÍN: *EL BRUJO*

etter known as *El Brujo* – 'The Warlock' – Dámaso Rodríguez Martín was active on the island of Tenerife in the 1980s. He was considered the Canary Islands' most infamous killer and was, at one time, Spain's most wanted man.

Born on 11 December 1944, Dámaso was one of five brothers and the family lived at Las Montañas – 'The Mountains' – in the village of El Batán, a district of San Cristóbal de La Laguna, the island's second most populous city, which lay at the northern end of the island. While the family was poor, his parents Martín Rodríguez Silveria and Celestina Martín Perdomo struggled to give him a good education, though this was difficult due to the strictures of the Catholic Church and the fascist government under the dictator General Francisco Franco. Before the era of mass tourism, the island was impoverished and there were few opportunities. Many inhabitants emigrated to Cuba or other parts of Latin America. This was not an option presented to Dámaso. As a teenager, he was already in trouble with the law. At the age of 17, he was arrested for theft and spent a year in jail.

On his release in 1963, he joined the Spanish Foreign Legion, whose former leader was General Franco. It was stationed in the small Spanish enclaves on the coast of North Africa left after the independence of Morocco. He was sent to the Western Sahara, whose decolonization both Morocco and the United Nations were demanding.

After his discharge from the service in 1966, Rodríguez returned to Tenerife, where he married Mercedes Martín Rodríguez the following year. They settled in Las Mercedes, another district of San Cristóbal de La Laguna. Their first child was born in 1973, their second in 1975.

Unhealthy curiosity

Rodríguez was a voyeur. On 11 November 1981, he was watching a couple making love in a car in the district of El Moquinal. But this was not enough for him. He intervened and killed the young man and beat and raped his girlfriend, with her boyfriend's dead body in the car beside them. He drove her and the body out to Llano de los Viejos – 'Plain of the Old' – a forested area outside the town, where he abandoned them.

Investigators from the national police began asking around for a violent criminal who knew the mountains and stalked courting couples during the night. As San Cristóbal de La Laguna had a relatively small population, it did not take them long to discover that the perpetrator was Dámaso Rodríguez. He was arrested, tried and convicted of murder, rape, theft of a firearm and unlawful possession of weapons. Aged 37, he was sentenced to 55 years in jail, so he would not have been released until the age of 92.

After more than nine years in jail, he escaped on 17 January 1991 and fled to the Anaga, a mountainous region to the west of San Cristóbal de La Laguna where he could hide out. On the way, he visited his home with the intention of murdering his wife who had shunned him after he had gone to jail. However, he found her with family and friends, denying him the opportunity.

The odd symbol found in Rodríguez's house.

A week later, on 23 January, the body of German tourist Karl Flick was found on a forest road leading to the village of El Solís. The next day, at 3.15pm, in a remote area of the Roque de El Moquinal, the Civil Guard recovered the body of Flick's wife, Marta Küpper, who had been raped and strangled. They appeared to have been begging for their lives before he killed them.

Rodríguez then went on a crime spree of robbery, theft and at least one sexual assault of a woman. The Carnival of Santa Cruz de Tenerife, the Canary Islands' rival to the carnival in Rio, was about to begin and it was feared that the fugitive would escape in costume.

On 19 February, a family moving into a house in the area found that the door had been forced open and called the police. When a sergeant in the *Guardia Civil* tried to enter the house, he was met with shotgun fire. A gunfight broke out. Outgunned, Rodríguez tried to kill himself by lodging the barrel of the shotgun under his chin and pulling the trigger with his toe. But the gun was too long and his suicide bid failed. There was more gunfire, but his second attempt at suicide succeeded.

Once he was dead, a strange symbol was found etched on the wall of the house in Anaga. It comprised a circle inside a triangle, inside another circle with strange symbols and indecipherable writing. It was thought to be magical and earned him the nickname of *El Brujo* – The Warlock or Witch Doctor.

NESTOR PIROTTE: THE CRAZY KILLER

Known as *Le tueur fou* – 'The Crazy Killer' – Nestor Pirotte passed himself off as an aristocrat. Before child-killer Marc Dutroux came along in the 1990s, Nestor Pirotte was Belgium's most-feared serial killer. Having dodged the death sentence twice, Pirotte repeatedly escaped to kill again. Feared by the whole country, he was loathed by his family and buried in an unmarked grave.

Born in 1933, Pirotte was the son of Léon, the gamekeeper at the Château de Beau Chêne, so the family lived in the gatehouse of the huge estate. His mother Florence Delvaux was a notorious beauty and a seamstress who dressed in aristocratic-style clothes of her own making. It was from her that the young Pirotte inherited his upper-class pretensions. From an early age, he boasted of being the illegitimate son of a neighbouring squire. His mother did not deny it.

Living on the estate, he played with the children of the château and picked up the manners and demeanour of the Belgian nobility. During his military service, he boasted of his aristocratic origins to seduce women. To keep up the pretence, he needed money, which he stole from his comrades. Then he was caught embezzling the mess funds. This earned him a three-month suspended prison sentence at the age of 20.

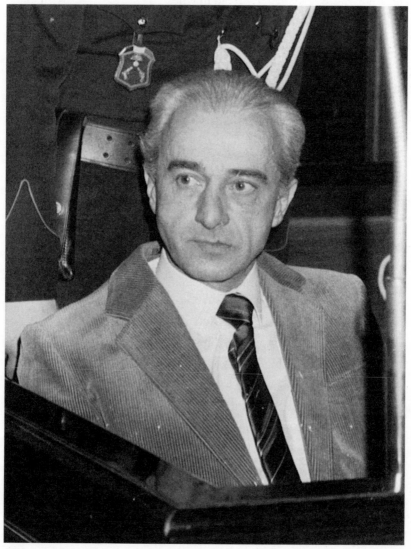

Nestor Pirotte.

He wanted to buy himself a Vespa scooter, so he could woo the belles at local balls. Learning that one of his great-aunts had sold her herd of cows, he asked her for cash. She refused, having already spent the money on a new herd. Carrying an iron bar with him, he hid behind the stables and smashed her head in when she came by. Searching her house, he only found a few hundred Belgian francs, worth less than £20 in today's money.

The following day, a neighbour stumbled upon her body. Hens were pecking at the bits of brain scattered on the ground. It was clear who had done it. A few days earlier, a gendarme had seen Pirotte hiding in a thicket watching his great-aunt's movements and warned him: 'Nestor, you will be arrested if any crime occurs in the region.'

Still in the service, he was tried in a military court, where his father Léon collapsed in tears. His mother, though, appeared 'cold and haughty'. One of the guards said: 'She was dressed like a duchess going to a gala evening.'

Conman and imposter

In October 1955, he was sentenced to death for murder. Although the death penalty was still officially on the statute book in Belgium, it was automatically commuted to life imprisonment. But Pirotte did not want to stay in prison and decided to pass himself off as mentally ill. He overdosed on barbiturates and bragged about deviant sexual practices. But the psychiatrist who examined him saw through the deception. Pirotte was not about to give up though. After feigning repeated bouts of hysteria, he was transferred to the showcase psychiatric facility at Tournai. There he exercised his charm, wit and storytelling ability, and after 14 years he was released.

Although he was judged to be sane, he still had the delusion that he was a wealthy aristocrat. He styled himself variously the Comte de Meeûs, the Comte de Larivoisière and the Comte de Leidekerque.

But he used the name the Comte de Ribeaucourt when he made an appointment at the branch of the BBL bank in Genval on 14 May 1968 on the pretext of negotiating a large loan. He shot the bank manager at point-blank range and made off with the money. He only had time to buy a fancy gold watch before being arrested and imprisoned a few days later.

In prison, he tried to escape, using a rope to scale a six-metre wall. When he was caught, he threw himself off, pretending he was making a suicide attempt. This got him sent back to the psychiatric facility at Tournai.

After 11 years, he was released again and went to work in a radio and television shop in Verviers. But soon he went back to his old ways. He bought a luxury car, charmed women with his old tales of his aristocratic heritage and got involved in dubious business deals. But soon he had run out of money. He bought a .38 revolver and came up with a story about stealing gold bars worth three million Belgian francs. When his attempt to extort money out of his mistress, Madeleine Humbert, and her two employees failed, their bodies were found in the restaurant 'La Vieille France' in Spa on 11 December 1980, along with that of a dog. The restaurant's owner's son was missing. His body was found the following month.

The name of the last customer on the slate at the restaurant was 'Nestor'. But this was not evidence enough. With all the witnesses dead, the police had trouble building a case against him. However, Pirotte was soon arrested in Brussels for violating the conditions of his parole and was sent back to jail. But, on the night of 2 August 1981, he escaped. The news sent the public into a panic.

In an attempt to make himself look more aristocratic, he curled his hair and dyed it red, the fashion at the time. Calling himself the Comte de Meeûs d'Argenteuil, he told an antique dealer that he wanted to sell some furniture and convinced the man to follow him through a wood to a make-believe castle with the intent of robbing him. But the antique dealer had not brought any money with him, so Pirotte shot him in the chest.

His plea of not guilty by reason of insanity was thrown out by the court. Again, he was sentenced to death, which was once more automatically commuted to life imprisonment. Renewed attempts to escape failed and he died behind bars on 29 July 2000. None of his family had visited him since he had been locked up again. Seeking anonymity, they had moved away. The only mourner at his funeral was a woman he had known in his youth. His grave in the cemetery of Ham-sur-Heure is marked only by a wooden cross with no name on it and a small pile of pebbles.

JAMES MILLER:
THE TRURO MURDERER

'The Truro Murderer', James Miller, who was from and operated in South Australia, was a strange serial killer as he did not lay a finger on the victims, at least not while they were alive. The actual killing was done by his lover and partner in crime Chris Worrell. Yet Miller was given up to six consecutive life sentences and died in jail after serving 28 years.

Miller was just 11 when he was sent to a reform school. With no formal education, he resorted to stealing for a living and sometimes worked as an itinerant labourer. By the time he met Worrell in jail, he had clocked up more than 30 convictions, including breaking and entering and robbery. He was serving three months in an Adelaide jail for breaking into a gun shop when he shared a cell with Worrell, who was on remand for rape. He already had a two-year suspended sentence for armed robbery.

When they got out, they shared a flat and worked together on a labouring gang for Unley council. Miller said this was the best time of his life. He was infatuated with Worrell and would perform oral sex on him while Worrell perused bondage magazines. However, Worrell preferred having sex with women. Handsome and charming, he had no trouble picking them up. Miller would drive him around cheap hotels, bus stops and train stations looking for prey. Then he would drive Worrell and his latest conquest to a remote spot and go for a walk while the couple had sex. Sometimes Worrell would tie the women up, but he released them afterwards.

Everything changed on 23 December 1976 when they spotted 18-year-old Veronica Knight in a shopping centre. She had become separated from a friend while doing last-minute Christmas shopping and accepted a lift from Worrell and Miller. They drove her out to the foothills near Adelaide. When Miller returned from his walk, he found that Worrell had raped and murdered her. Miller said that Worrell pulled a knife and threatened to kill him if he did not help dispose of the body, which they dumped in a wooded area near Truro, 50 miles northeast of Adelaide. Worrell was in a black mood after the killing, but was his old self by the time they went back to work again the next morning.

To kill and kill again

They were out together again on 2 January 1977, when Worrell picked up 15-year-old hitch-hiker Tania Kenny. They drove to Miller's sister's house. No one was home. Miller waited in the car, while Worrell and Tania went inside. Worrell came out and asked for Miller's help. Inside, he found Tania dead, wearing just a shirt, bound with rope and with a plaster over her mouth. Again, Miller helped Worrell dispose of the body in a shallow grave behind a rifle range in Wingfield.

On 21 January, they picked up 16-year-old Juliet Mykyta. When Worrell tried to tie her up, she resisted, but he overpowered her. Miller got out of the car. He was a little way down the road when he heard voices. He turned to see that Juliet had somehow freed herself and had got out of the car. Worrell gave chase, felled her and began strangling her with a rope. Miller said he tried to stop Worrell killing her, but he was too strong. They dumped her body out near Truro too, covering it with leaves and branches.

On 6 February, Worrell picked up 16-year-old Sylvia Pittman at Adelaide Station. They drove her to the Windang area. Miller went for his usual walk. When he returned, Sylvia's body lay under a blanket on the back seat. She had been strangled with her own tights.

The following day, Worrell picked up 26-year-old Vicki Howell at Adelaide's main post office and asked Miller to meet him there. Miller said he thought that Worrell would not murder Vicki as she was older than the others. He was wrong. He strangled her on the back seat of the car. Miller was furious and asked Worrell why he had done it. He offered no excuse and simply told Miller to drive to Truro, where they dumped the body.

Two days later, on 9 February, they did a U-turn in the street to ask 16-year-old Connie Iordanides, aka Connie Jordan, if she wanted a lift home. But she grew fearful when they drove off in the wrong direction. After they parked up, Worrell forced the screaming girl into the back seat of the car. Once more, Miller walked away. When he returned, Connie had been strangled and raped. Again, her body was dumped near Truro.

In the early hours of Sunday 12 February, they picked up 20-year-old hitch-hiker Deborah Lamb. Worrell suggested that they take her to Port Gawler and the girl allegedly accepted the ride. Once they reached the beach there, Miller left them alone and went for a walk in the scrub. When he returned to the car, Worrell was standing in front of it, filling in a hole by pushing sand into it with his feet. Deborah had been strangled with her own tights, which had been wrapped around her mouth and jaw seven times. She had possibly been alive when they buried her as sand and shell grit was found in her lungs when her body was recovered.

Terrible crash

A week later, they were out with Deborah Skuse, girlfriend of a man Worrell and Miller had known in jail. She and her boyfriend had split up, so, to cheer her up, Worrell and Miller suggested taking her to Mount Gambier, but Worrell became moody and they returned early. Worrell had been drinking and was driving recklessly. There was an accident. The car turned over and Worrell and Debbie Skuse were killed. Miller survived, but injured his shoulder and was taken to hospital with shock.

He was distraught. His one and only friend was dead. At the funeral, Worrell's girlfriend Amelia mentioned that she thought he had had a blood clot on his brain. This prompted Miller to tell her about Worrell's thrill-killing, suggesting the clot was responsible for the moods that had led him to kill. Miller confessed his part in the crimes.

'I did the driving and went along to make sure that nothing went wrong,' he told Amelia. 'They had to be done in, so they would not point the finger at us. If you don't believe me, I will take you to where they are. It was getting worse lately. It was happening more often. It was perhaps a good thing that Chris died.'

Not only had Worrell killed around Adelaide in South Australia, he also told Amelia that Worrell had 'done away with two in WA' – Western Australia. Disbelieving, she kept quiet about what Miller had told her for another two years.

'I only had suspicions, but suspicions are not enough to go to the police,' she said. 'I had no facts. I suspected that it was the truth and I didn't want to go to the police.'

Gruesome discovery

On 20 April 1978, a young man was out looking for mushrooms in the bush around Truro when he found what he took to be the leg bone of a cow. When he returned with his wife five days later, they found that there was a shoe attached to the leg and the toenails had been painted with nail varnish. Bloody clothes were found nearby. The body was that of a young woman, later identified as Veronica Knight.

Almost a year later, bushwalkers found the body of Sylvia Pittman about half a mile way. The police noted that five other women had gone missing from Adelaide at around the same time, so they searched the whole area. They found the bodies of Vicki Howell and Connie Iordanides, but they were badly decayed and provided few clues.

The police put out an appeal for help, offering a reward of A$30,000. They were contacted by Amelia, though she initially called herself Angela to disguise her identity. She said that she had a friend called James Miller who said he and Worrell had dumped the bodies near Blanchetown and had only made the connection when a map of where the bodies had been found was printed in the newspaper. He had told her, she said, that the victims 'were only rags and weren't worth much' and that one of them had actually enjoyed being raped and murdered.

Miller was tracked down to a shelter for the homeless. He denied knowing Amelia – until he was confronted with a photograph showing the two of them together. They were pictured with Worrell. Even then, he said that Amelia was lying and insisted she was only after the reward. Then he had second thoughts and said: 'Maybe she's done what I should do. Can I have a few minutes to think about it?'

During six hours of questioning, Miller told the police that Worrell had committed each of the murders, but he was not to blame.

'I drove around with Chris and we picked up girls around the city,' he said. 'Chris would talk to the girls and get them into the car and we would take them for a drive and take them to Truro and Chris would rape them and kill them. But you've got to believe that I had nothing to do with the actual killings of those girls.'

Miller said he was powerless to do otherwise as he was hopelessly in love with Worrell. Then, he said: 'There's three more. I'll show you.'

That night, Miller was driven under heavy escort to Truro, Port Gawler and the Wingfield dumpsite where he pointed out the locations of the remains of three more girls – Debbie Lamb who had been engaged to be married, Julie Mykyta who had been on her way home and Connie Jordan who had been waiting for a friend to go to the movies.

At his trial in February 1980, Miller pleaded not guilty to seven counts of murder. It did not wash. The prosecution argued that, after the first killing, he must had known what was going to happen. At any time, he could have gone to the police, so it was his fault that the following six of the young women were dead.

In the eyes of the law, Miller was involved in a joint venture with Worrell, so was equally culpable. However, he was found not guilty of the murder of the first victim, Veronica Knight. The jury agreed that he did not know that Worrell intended to murder her. He was given six life sentences.

In July 1984, Miller was interviewed in prison after a 43-day hunger strike.

'Chris Worrell was my best friend in the world,' he said. 'If he had lived, maybe 70 would have been killed. And I wouldn't have ever dobbed [grassed] him in.'

In late 1999, James Miller applied to have a non-parole period set in the hope that one day he might be released. On 8 February 2000, Chief Justice John Doyle of the South Australian Supreme Court granted Miller a non-parole period of 35 years from the date of his arrest. He would have been eligible for parole in 2015, but he died of terminal cancer in 2008, one of Australia's longest-serving prisoners.

LINDSEY ROBERT ROSE: HITMAN

If you are going to be a hitman, you need to be cool, calm and calculating. The last thing you need is a big mouth. But Lindsey Robert Rose had got away with at least five murders over ten years and was not even a suspect until a corrupt police officer, an associate of Rose, told detectives in New South Wales that he had boasted of at least two murders. That was the beginning of his downfall.

Born Lindsey Robert Lehman in North Sydney, Australia in 1955, his parents separated before he was born and he took the surname Rose from his stepfather after his mother remarried. He served an apprenticeship as a fitter and turner before joining the New South Wales ambulance service in 1976. The following year, he was one of the first responders at the Granville Train Disaster when 84 people died and 213 were injured.

He quit the ambulance service in 1979 to become a licensed private eye. This was largely a cover for his criminal career. His beginnings in the business were shady enough, then on 20 January 1984, he broke into the home of Edward John 'Bill' Cavanagh in Sydney's Hoxton Park and shot him dead, ostensibly for beating up one of Rose's friends a few years earlier. Rose also killed Cavanagh's girlfriend, Carmelita Lee, so there would be no witnesses.

The truth was this was a gangland hit. Cavanagh was running a trucking business with drugs baron Robert Trimbole who was later accused of organizing the contract killing of anti-drugs campaigner Donald Mackay by a Royal Commission. The Honourable Justice Philip Woodward presiding found that Trimbole was in charge of the production of marijuana in Griffith and had set Mackay up by luring him to the town of Jerilderie.

'The disposal of Mackay was the result of an organized plan,' he said. 'He was disposed of by the organization which I find existed in Griffith. I am satisfied that the appointment to meet Mackay at Jerilderie was part of a plan to ambush and dispose of him.'

Drug baron

Born to Calabrian parents, Trimbole lived in a mansion in Griffith known as the 'Grass Castle', no doubt a reference to the fact that he was the godfather of the marijuana trade. Mackay disappeared from a hotel car park after having drinks with friends. His body has never been found. At the scene of his disappearance, his locked van had bloodstains on the door, wheel rim, mudguard and tyre, and his car keys, and three spent .22 casings were found. Tipped off about his impending arrest, Trimbole fled, dying in Spain in 1987.

Three years after the murders of Bill Cavanagh and Carmelita Lee, Rose was burgling the home of wealthy businessman, William 'Bill' Graf, in the Sydney suburb of West Ryde. He was disturbed by Graf's girlfriend, Reynette Holford. Before making his escape, he stabbed her over 30 times with a vegetable knife and a screwdriver, leaving her tied up. She died from her injuries. Again, no inconvenient witnesses remained.

Then, on 14 February 1994, Rose shot and killed Fatma Ozonal, then shot and stabbed to death his former lover Kerrie Pang at Pang's massage parlour, 'Kerrie's Oasis', in Gladesville, New South Wales. Knowing that Pang would not let him in, Rose offered Ronald Waters A$500 to knock on the door, so he could gain entry. The murder had been ordered by Pang's partner, Mark Lewis, because of difficulties in their relationship and Lewis did not like the line of work she was in. Rose disliked Pang too. Ozonal was not part of the murder plan and was simply in the wrong place at the wrong time.

Terrible truth

After the police came to question Rose in 1996, he disappeared. Detectives flew from Sydney to Perth where his wife then lived after leaving Sydney three years earlier. His 12-year-old daughter Elisha was also questioned about what she remembered of her father and the contact they'd had in recent years. Later, she discovered the truth on the nightly news.

'I learnt my father was accused of murder as I knelt on the mat in our lounge room, watching the Sydney evening news that was aired late at night in Perth,' she said. 'I remember the burnt orange-patterned curtains that hung on either side of the TV. I remember holding on to the old steamer trunk that belonged to my great-great-grandmother that served the dual purpose of coffee table and as storage for my old baby clothes. Most of all, I remember being in utter disbelief, in a truly life-changing shock.'

Soon afterwards, she and her mother had another visit from the police.

'On this occasion, I was told that there had been threats to kill me as an act of vengeance against my father,' Elisha said. 'I would enter witness protection. I was given emergency phone numbers. My mum made special arrangements with school. I was not to be left alone.'

Rose had left Sydney and made for Adelaide in South Australia, where he found work under his original name Lehman. He was on the run for 40 weeks until a member of the public recognized him from a mugshot shown on TV news.

'My father was ultimately arrested after nearly 12 months on the run,' said Elisha. 'He announced to his colleagues at a dredging project in Adelaide that he wouldn't be at work that day as he was handcuffed and dragged away by police and the tactical response group.'

Returned to New South Wales, he pleaded guilty to five murders. Described as 'an absolute clinical psychopath', he was sentenced to five consecutive life sentences without the possibility of parole. Later, he was given another 40 years after confessing to conspiracy to pervert the course of justice, malicious wounding, larceny, supplying a prohibited drug, robbery, kidnapping and robbery while armed. On New Year's Day in 1983, Rose and criminal associates had hijacked a semi-trailer containing cigarettes valued at A$600,000 and held two truck drivers hostage for several hours.

Mark Lewis was later sentenced to life imprisonment plus 18 years without the possibility of parole for the murder of Pang and the manslaughter of Ozonal. Waters pleaded guilty to being an accessory to murder and was sentenced to 18 months' periodic detention.

Rose was one of the first six inmates of Goulburn Gaol's High Risk Management Unit after it was opened in 2001. He complained about the number of inmates converting to Islam and the lack of educational opportunities, particularly after prisoners were deprived of the use of computers. Rose was one of several inmates who had smuggled out 'letters of complaint' against a range of conditions at the jail. It said that education was 'virtually non-existent in the HRMU [High Risk Management Unit] ... Many inmates do not complete courses as they are thwarted by perfunctory teachers or ridiculous decisions ... Example: An inmate in another part of the prison is caught with contraband on a computer, the department of corrective services ban all computers, effectively putting inmates back to the Stone Age.'

For his daughter, Elisha Rose, the suffering went on.

'Life continued despite the upheaval, except that I carried a secret with me everywhere – my father killed five people,' she said.

She studied law at university, and then went on to specialize in criminal justice. In an attempt to understand her father, she wrote letters to him in jail and even visited him. But she couldn't shake off the feeling that it was somehow her duty to try and atone for what her father had done.

'I felt an immeasurable weight on my shoulders and like I owed a debt to society far beyond the usual karmic balance one must try to keep even,' Ms Rose told ABC's *Australian Story*. 'The harder I tried to understand my father's actions and to make sense of my life, the more complex and intricate the puzzle became. I visited my father and exchanged letters with him, read books on forensic psychology, attended counselling and eventually completed a Masters in Criminal Justice. The only thing that made sense to me for a long time was that my father had created an imbalance in this world by killing innocent people; my duty was to balance the scales. No matter that the debt was not mine, I knew I had to right his wrongs.'

The last time she saw her father was in April 2009. On the same trip to the Goulburn Supermax prison, she was admitted to the Supreme Court of New South Wales. It was then that she discovered that she could never accept her father's excuses for his actions, she said.

She established herself as a litigation lawyer in Perth and involved herself in charity work. 'The older I became, the more I understood about life, the deeper the secret about my father was buried. A few of my nearest and dearest friends knew of my father, but I had no idea how to navigate the reveal to my wider circle of friends and colleagues,' she said. 'There is no social convention for announcing your father killed five people and never quite the right time to drop it into conversation.'

Twenty years after Rose had been convicted, Elisha was approached by an author who was writing a book about her father's crimes and took the opportunity to finally unburden herself. Author Campbell McConachie had known her father. They had met in a bar in Sydney and he knew a little about his colourful past, but nothing of the murders.

In Supermax prison, McConachie conducted 25 interviews with Rose about his crimes and his life. Rose told him he trusted him to tell his story properly and took issue with his previous portrayal as a hitman. The book is called *The Fatalist*.

DEREK ERNEST PERCY: SADISTIC PAEDOPHILE

Derek Ernest Percy was unusual for a serial killer. He was only charged with one murder – that of 12-year-old Yvonne Elizabeth Tuohy – and found not guilty by reason of insanity. On 7 April 1970, he was sentenced to be detained indefinitely in prison at 'the pleasure of the Governor General', a ruling designed to protect the public as it was clear that he had murdered a series of other children and, given the opportunity, was likely to do so again.

Even when this indeterminate sentence was abolished in Australia in 1998, Percy was still not released, or even transferred to a mental hospital as it was considered that he was not mentally ill, but rather had a personality disorder that was considered untreatable.

Dr Stephens, co-ordinator of forensic psychiatry services at Pentridge Prison in Melbourne where he was held, wrote in 1984 that Percy was 'a highly dangerous, sadistic paedophile who should never be released from safe custody', continuing, 'he is not certifiable, neither is he psychiatrically treatable and he is totally unsuited to a mental institution.'

Reviewing the case in Victoria's Supreme Court in 1998, Judge Geoffrey Eames refused to set a minimum sentence for Percy or a release date, despite Percy having served the 25-year term that was the state norm for insane criminals. Eames said that Percy had never been treated for his sadistic paedophilia and nor had he sought treatment.

'He has demonstrated no significant remorse or anxiety, at least none which I find credible, as to the circumstances which caused him to kill,' Justice Eames added.

In March 2004, Percy's application to be transferred to a psychiatric hospital was turned down by Judge Murray Kellam as he was not convinced that Percy didn't still have dangerous sexual fantasies about killing children, so he could not be allowed out of a maximum-security facility.

Later that year, Percy began a one-to-one sex offenders' programme in the hope that he might, one day, qualify for parole. But political opposition ensured that the parole board would never allow it. When he died of cancer in prison on 24 July 2013, Percy was the longest-serving prisoner in the state of Victoria. Still in a state of denial, he took the details of his killings to the grave with him.

Sexually explicit diaries

That he had murdered Yvonne Tuohy was beyond dispute. She had been at Ski Beach in the small town of Warneet in Western Port Bay, Victoria, on 27 July 1969 with her friend, 11-year-old Shane Spiller. Percy, then a 21-year-old naval rating, grabbed Tuohy and put a knife to her neck. He probably would have abducted Spiller as well, but the boy was carrying a tomahawk and waved it at Percy as he approached.

Percy drove off with Tuohy. Spiller told the police that the car was a Datsun station wagon with a small navy insignia in the back window. This led them to HMAS *Cerberus*, the Royal Australian Navy's training base nearby. Three hours later, they found him there washing blood from his clothes, though he had been on weekend leave. In his locker, they discovered handwritten, sexually explicit diaries describing his urges to sexually abuse, torture, murder and mutilate children. They also found drawings of naked children and women. This led them to believe they were dealing with a serial killer.

Another Warneet child, ten-year-old Sue Williams, had a lucky escape. Tuohy and Spiller invited her to join them at the beach, but she insisted she would have lunch first, then catch up. 'It probably saved my life,' she said. Percy's diaries showed that he intended to abduct two or three children at a time.

The memory of what he had done seemed to be quickly receding from the killer's mind, but Detective Sergeant Richard Knight, who had completed a course in hypnotism, took Percy through the process in reverse, allowing the police to find Yvonne Tuohy's body where he had dumped it six miles from the beach. She had been molested, tortured and murdered. Her bathing costume had cuts around the crotch area and there were injuries to her genitals, deep cuts to her throat and her mouth was packed with fabric and paper in a way described in Percy's notebooks.

Detective Bernie Delaney, another of the homicide investigators who charged Percy over the Tuohy murder, had no doubt Percy's apparent inability to remember was fake.

'When we first interviewed him, he denied it, then he said he could have done it but couldn't remember,' he said, 'and then he eventually took us to the scene in the dark on a drizzly July night. His "I can't remember" line was the perfect ploy, and so he never changed it.'

Veteran prison psychiatrist, Dr Allen Bartholomew, described Percy as 'the nearest thing to a robot I have ever met', adding: 'His behaviour is above reproach, but what goes on in his mind I have no idea.'

Another expert said: 'He volunteered nothing, and extracting information was like pulling teeth.'

Child murders and abductions

Over the four years before the murder of Yvonne Tuohy, there had been a spate of child murders and abductions. Christine Sharrock and Marianne Schmidt, both 15, were murdered on Sydney's Wanda Beach on 11 January 1965. Nine-year-old Jane Beaumont, her seven-year-old sister Anna and four-year-old Grant disappeared from Glenelg Beach near Adelaide on 26 January 1966. Six-year-old Allen Redston was murdered in Canberra on 28 September 1966. Three-year-old Simon Brook was killed in Sydney on 18 May 1968. And seven-year-old Linda Stilwell was abducted from the St Kilda foreshore in Melbourne on 10 August 1968.

In all these unsolved cases, a man answering to Percy's description had been seen nearby, or there was evidence that Percy had been in the vicinity. Also there had been an attempted abduction of a 12-year-old girl near the *Cerberus* base on 1 April 1969. The victim identified Percy after his arrest.

Detective Knight had already concluded that the murder of Yvonne Tuohy was not Percy's first attack and took the unusual decision to put a rookie cop on the case. The young policeman had been on the force for just six months, but he had been at school with Percy. Sobbing, Percy told him: 'Looks like I've f***ed up this time.'

Asked if there were others, Percy said, typically: 'I can't remember.'

The rookie cop pressed on. 'Well look, Derek, I'll ask you about some of the ones that I know about,' he said. 'You don't have to say anything. If you remember, I will jot it down and it could be used in court.'

Asked about Linda Stilwell, Percy made a telling admission.

'Yes,' he said. 'I drove through St Kilda that day. I had been at *Cerberus* in the afternoon and was driving along the esplanade on the way to the White Ensign Club for some drinks.'

When asked if he killed her, he said: 'Possibly, I don't remember a thing about it.'

Derek Percy.

Percy also admitted to being in Sydney on the day Simon Brook was killed. He had been giving his brother a lift to work and had driven past the spot where the body was found.

Did he remember killing him? 'I wish I could. I might have. I just don't remember,' Percy said.

Asked if he was in Adelaide when the Beaumont children, Jane, Anna and Grant, went missing, he said: 'I don't know.' He was then asked if he was blocking out thoughts 'because something horrible happened in Adelaide and you don't want to remember it?' He said it was possible.

He also said he could not remember if he had killed the children and volunteered no further information. Nevertheless, over the years, cold-case investigations have turned up other evidence that points to Percy as the perpetrator in all these cases.

Never had a girlfriend

Derek Ernest Percy was born on 15 September 1948 in Strathfield, New South Wales. He was the eldest son of a railway electrician, who moved his young family to Warrnambool on the coast of Victoria. Father and son shared a passion for sailing. The Percys took caravan holidays, often travelling interstate to yachting competitions in their V8 Studebaker.

In 1961, they moved on to Mount Beauty, near Bright in Victoria. Derek went to Mount Beauty High School where he had few friends. He wore a green-and-gold striped tie like the other pupils, but his was made from a cheaper, coarser fabric, and he was teased.

He had few friends. One of them was a local farmer's boy who had also just moved to town. Interviewed by the police a decade later, he said: 'One thing that stood out about Derek was that he was very intelligent. Most or nearly all of us at school had to work and study very hard but not Derek.' He also noted that Percy was shy and never had a girlfriend.

Banned by his parents from playing football, Percy would some-times borrow his friend's kit, convincing his mate's mother to wash the clothes, so his parents wouldn't know. It was said that his parents were overprotective as one of his younger brothers had died of diphtheria aged just ten months. Derek might have been the eldest of the three surviving sons, but his younger siblings were given their freedom, while their mother kept him on a tighter rein.

'Derek had to get permission to go anywhere with us outside of school hours and she would question his intentions,' his younger brother said.

He earned his pocket money working in the tobacco fields, saving up to buy a second-hand bicycle with 'ram's horn' handlebars. He also carried a sharp pocket-knife, which was not unusual in the countryside of Victoria. One day he was helping a friend make running repairs on the sole of his shoe during a handball game.

'I remember Derek getting his pocket-knife out and telling me that he would cut it off,' said the friend. 'Derek began to cut the sole off my shoe and, all of a sudden, the blade went into Derek's left thigh about three-quarters of an inch. The blade went deeply into his thigh and I recoiled in surprise.

'I was amazed that Derek just looked fascinated with what had happened. He didn't scream, cry or really show any sort of emotion that you would expect from someone with a knife in their leg. I thought his reaction was extremely odd. He seemed happy about it.'

The 'snowdropper'

In 1964 in Mount Beauty, Percy began stealing women's underwear from washing lines. The local newspaper nicknamed the culprit 'the snowdropper'. He was also suspected of being a peeping Tom. Until then, he had been doing well at school, but his grades began dropping, though he had an IQ of 122.

Out near a local swimming pond, two teenagers saw what they thought was a girl in a petticoat. It turned out to be Percy in a stolen negligee. He then began slashing at the clothing and stabbed at the crotch in a similar way to what he would do to Yvonne Tuohy.

'I would describe Derek's eyes as being full of excitement, a glazed look, but I recall there was something very cold and sinister in the look,' one of the teenagers told police later.

Underwear and dresses were stolen from the wardrobes of two little girls who lived next door. Some were found under bushes along with one of their dolls, whose eyes had been 'blinded', and pictures of women in bikinis, whose eyes had been scribbled over with pencil and whose bodies were slashed with a razor blade.

In his entry in the Mount Beauty school magazine, Percy said his favourite saying was: 'It depends.' Perpetual occupation: 'Isolating myself.' Ambition: 'Playboy.' Probable fate: 'Bachelor.' Pet aversion: 'Girls.'

Despite his high IQ, he failed his exams. When his family moved to Khancoban, the snowdropping stopped in Mount Beauty and began again there. Things took a more serious turn when he lured a six-year-old girl into the family caravan and sexually assaulted her. Her father took the matter up with Derek's dad, who was already worried about his son after finding him dressed in women's clothing. It was also found he was committing bizarre and violent sexual fantasies to paper, a practice he would continue for the rest of his life. More deviant ramblings were found by his grandmother and burnt. Typically, for a serial killer, he had tortured animals as a child. It was recommended that he visit a psychologist, but he failed to do so.

Having dropped out of school, he went to work at a service station his father had bought. This did not work out and in 1967 he joined the Navy, graduating at the top of his entry class. But it was soon found that he wasn't suitable officer material. One could see why.

Tim Attrill, who served with Percy in the Navy and later became a police inspector, described him as 'one of the most intelligent people I've met. He is cold, without emotion, and looks straight through you with his crazy eyes.'

Some 40 years later, the police pieced together the details of his family holidays which showed he was near the places where children had been abducted and murdered in the late 1960s.

Matching the photo-fit

On 11 January 1965, teenagers Marianne Schmidt and Christine Sharrock had gone to Sydney's popular Cronulla Beach area with Marianne's four younger siblings. After a picnic, the younger children stayed in a sheltered area at Wanda Beach, while the two 15-year-olds went off. Marianne's two younger brothers saw them talking to a fair-haired youth who was carrying a spear and had a knife in a sheath. The girls' mutilated bodies were found the next day, partially buried near a sand dune.

As in the Tuohy case, the victims had been taken from the beach and their bodies dumped nearby. The crotch area of one of the girls' swimming costumes had been cut, just as Percy had been seen slashing female underwear at Mount Beauty a few weeks earlier.

Neighbours confirmed that the Percys had visited Sydney for a holiday that summer. They had gone to attend the national yachting regatta at Botany Bay Yachting Club, which was near Wanda Beach. Percy's grandparents lived a short distance from the West Ryde railway station where the two girls had caught the train on their way to the beach.

After police arrested Percy, they found the diary that described his urges to sexually abuse, torture, murder and mutilate children. In it, he had written that he would force his victims to drink beer. Christine Sharrock's post-mortem showed that she had a blood-alcohol level equivalent to drinking about half a pint of beer. He also wrote about abducting and killing 'two girls at Barnsley', a beach in northern New South Wales. Police believe this was code for Wanda Beach.

When Percy started a new school that year, a classmate spotted his resemblance to the photo-fit released in the case of the two missing girls. Fellow students taunted him, saying: 'We know it was you that killed those girls in Sydney. You have the same haircut and we know you were there.'

At the suggestion, Percy went berserk and challenged them to a fight.

'The Ghost'

The day the Beaumont children went missing they were seen talking to a man at about 11am. Forty-five minutes later they bought a pie and two pastries with a A$1 note – which was more than the pocket money their mother had given them. Percy also wrote about giving children food before kidnapping and killing them. His brother confirmed that the family had been in Adelaide at that time. Their bodies had never been found. However, given his modus operandi, Percy remained a 'person of interest' in the case and was at the top of the police shortlist of suspects.

That summer, he forced his neighbours, Tania and Lynnette Harrison, to show him their genitals.

On 27 September 1966, six-year-old Allen Geoffrey Redston left his home in the Canberra suburb of Curtin to go to a nearby milk bar to buy an ice-cream. The next day his body was found in reeds by a local creek. The body was hog-tied and had plastic wrapped around the throat. In the days leading up to the murder, a fair-haired teenager had been play-fighting with boys, forcing them to the ground, tying them up and placing plastic bags over their heads in an apparent attempt to suffocate them.

Percy wrote about tying up victims and using plastic to asphyxiate them. Yvonne Tuohy was bound and gagged when she was found. When Percy was a child, as a punishment his grandmother would lock him in a room and hog-tie him the way Allen Redston's body had been.

The identikit composed from witness accounts closely resembled Percy and a man in the vicinity was seen riding a red bike with 'ram's horn' handlebars, exactly like the one Percy owned and took with him on caravan holidays. He admitted that the family were in Canberra at the time. They had a relative there. A green-and-gold striped tie made of a coarse cloth was found at the scene of the crime. Percy no longer needed his Mount Beauty tie as he had changed school.

In November 1967, Percy joined the Navy. On his electrical mechanics course, he was nicknamed 'The Ghost'. After three months in the Navy, he was posted to sentry duty on the aircraft carrier HMAS *Melbourne*, which was undergoing a refit in Cockatoo Dry Dock at Sydney Harbour. On his daily commute from the naval base on Garden Island where he was stationed, he passed through the suburb of Glebe. On 18 May 1968, three-year-old Simon Brook went missing from the front yard of his family home there. The house was next to Jubilee Park where a truck driver said he saw a boy matching Simon Brook's description holding hands with a young man. The identikit closely resembled Percy and had a neat haircut as would have been required by naval regulations.

The following day, the boy's body was found under a tree, half-naked and mutilated. Some of the wounds the killer had inflicted were similar to those suffered by Yvonne Tuohy and the two Gillette razor blades found at the scene were the same brand as those issued to sailors. In his diary, Percy wrote of abducting and killing a three-year-old child and detailed the exact injuries inflicted on Simon Brook. Detectives took this to be a virtual confession. When the inquest into

Simon Brook's death was reopened in 2005, Percy refused to give evidence on the grounds of self-incrimination. The coroner concluded that there was a 'reasonable prospect ... that a jury would convict a known person in relation to the offence'.

Percy had transferred to the troop ship HMAS *Sydney*, which was based in Melbourne, on 1 July 1968. On 5 August 1968, he took 18 days' leave. Five days later, seven-year-old Linda Stilwell's mother told her to go and find her brother and sister and bring them home for lunch. They returned without her. Two days later, a woman called to say that she had seen a girl matching Linda's description rolling down a grassy hill near Melbourne's Lower Esplanade. There was a man nearby wearing 'a deep navy blue, almost black, spray jacket, similar to that worn when sailing'.

After Percy was arrested for the Tuohy abduction and his picture was printed in the newspaper, the woman came forward again, saying that she was absolutely certain that Percy was the man she had seen in the spray jacket.

'I got the biggest shock of my life. This was the same man that was sitting on the park bench the day that the little Stilwell girl disappeared in St Kilda,' she said.

In the money

In the 44 years Percy was in jail, he was paid his Navy pension, amassing A$200,000, some of which he used to pay for his defence. He also paid for the storage of 35 boxes of newspaper articles on sex crimes, pictures of children, a video with a rape theme and handwritten stories on sex offences involving abduction and torture. Among them, police found a 1978 street directory with a line drawn through St Kilda Pier where Linda Stilwell was abducted and a pornographic lesbian cartoon on which Percy wrote the word 'Wanda' across the top.

There was one final unsung victim – Shane Spiller. He was just 11 when, after his friend Yvonne Tuohy was abducted, he was asked to pick out the man he had seen from a police line-up.

'I had to walk up and point right at his nose. The look he gave me. I can still remember it,' he said years later. He was plagued by the idea that, while he was still alive, Percy might one day be freed and come and get him.

'I was promised back then that he would never get out,' he said. 'I hope people don't forget what he was like and what he did. They always thought he'd killed others, but they weren't able to prove it.'

In 2000, Shane applied for criminal compensation. He was awarded A$5,000, which was increased to A$50,000 on appeal, the maximum that could be awarded under the criminal compensation scheme. Two years later, he disappeared from his house in the town of Wyndham, New South Wales, where he had lived for years. His car was still parked at the front and squatters had moved into the house.

A resident who knew him said: 'He was always saying someone was after him. No one knows what happened to him.'

A local publican said: 'He was really scared. He told me that one day he might just take off.'

Some believe that he was murdered for his compensation payout. He was, however, safe from Percy, who never got out.

PICTURE CREDITS